BEASTS AND BEHEMOTHS:

Prehistoric Creatures in the Movies

by
ROY KINNARD

The Scarecrow Press, Inc.
Metuchen, N.J., & London
1988

Kinnard, Roy, 1952-
    Beasts and behemoths.

    "Feature film checklist": p.
    "Japanese feature film checklist": p.
    Includes indexes.
    1. Prehistoric animals in motion pictures.
2. Horror films--History and criticism. I. Title.
PN1995.9.P67K56 1988)   791.43'09'0936   87-23424
ISBN 0-8108-2062-5

CONTENTS

Acknowledgments v

Introduction vii

iii

ACKNOWLEDGMENTS

The author wishes to thank the following individuals, each of whom contributed information and/or materials to this book:

Forrest J Ackerman

David Allen

Dick Andersen

Bob Andrews

Ed Bernds

Bob Burns

Lyle Conway

William K. Everson

Don Glut

Alex Gordon

Ted Okuda

Shirley Patterson

Jean Porter

Veto Stasiunaitus

Maurice Terenzio

George Turner

Tom White

Dorothy Wilson

Fay Wray

INTRODUCTION

Since the first prehistoric fossils were discovered and officially cataloged in the early nineteenth century, the public
has been fascinated by the extinct animals of earth's distant
past, especially the huge dinosaurs of the Mesozoic Era. Unlike other areas of science, paleontology (or at least its more
obvious aspects in the form of museum displays and recon-
structions of fossils) has always possessed a romantic allure.
Despite their bizarre, even alien appearance, dinosaurs and
other prehistoric animals were real; they actually trod the
earth. Regardless of the fact that no human being ever saw
a living specimen (the last dinosaurs were extinct millions of
years before the evolution of humans), these antediluvian
beasts have consistently exerted a hold on the public imagina-
tion.

Not surprisingly, Hollywood was quick to exploit the
box-office potential in the public's fascination, and almost
from the inception of motion pictures as a form of mass entertainment, there have been movies about dinosaurs and other
prehistoric creatures. It is certainly true that such films
are rarely scientifically accurate, with different species of
animals that never co-existed in the same time period shown
together onscreen, and the physical reconstruction of the
animals is sometimes erroneous, but these objections seem like
quibbling when directed at movies that aim solely to entertain. It is hardly reasonable to criticize a film like ONE
MILLION B.C. (1940) simply because primitive men and dinosaurs are shown within the same time frame, when the pri-
mary goal of such a movie is entertainment through heightened
dramatization.

In most cases, prehistoric movie monsters are used
mainly as a springboard for a fantastic plot; since the audience

THE BEAST FROM 20,000 FATHOMS: The animated monster blended into a live-action street scene via matte photography.

is already cognizant that dinosaurs actually existed, the presence of a movie dinosaur serves, in effect, to anchor the fictional proceedings in a base of reality. These stories usually exploit one of four basic plots:

1) The "lost world" theme, with explorers journeying to an area of the world previously hidden from civilization, where prehistoric animals still exist; best represented by THE LOST WORLD (1925) and KING KONG (1933).

2) The "revived monster" theme, in which a living dinosaur or other prehistoric creature is awakened from eons of suspended animation by man-made or natural causes, as in THE BEAST FROM 20,000 FATHOMS (1953) and GODZILLA, KING OF THE MONSTERS (1956).

3) The "time travel" theme, in which the human pro-

tagonists, whether by design or accident, travel backwards through time to prehistoric eras, as in JOURNEY TO THE BEGINNING OF TIME (1966).

4) The "prehistoric" story that is set in the past, best represented by ONE MILLION B.C. (1940).

Many of the films dealing with prehistory are entertaining, but few of them could be called good, even of their type, and only two or three have attained greatness trancending their genre, due to qualities other than their subject matter. However, what movies of this nature do offer in abundance is an opportunity to see Hollywood's craftsmanship at its most visually impressive, as studio technicians and artisans magically breathe life into creatures never beheld by human eyes. Four basic production techniques are used in these pictures:

1) Stop-motion animation. Simply explained, stop-motion involves the use of jointed miniature figures (articulated metal armatures with detailed latex or foam rubber "skins") representing the onscreen creatures; these are moved by precise increments and painstakingly photographed one frame at a time in miniature sets with painted or rear-projected backgrounds, until the desired action is achieved. Although some "strobing" or jerkiness is apparent due to the artificial motion, this process offers a high degree of control both in design and action, and when stop-motion is used in tandem with matte photography, or rear-projection, spectacular illusions can be achieved. The best examples are the work of Willis O'Brien in KING KONG (1933) and Ray Harryhausen in THE BEAST FROM 20,000 FATHOMS (1953).

2) Disguised animals. Actual lizards or other animals, disguised with rubber appliances, such as horns or fins, and photographed in slow motion in order to provide an illusion of size and bulk amidst miniature settings, as in ONE MILLION B.C (1940).

3) Costumed actors. Performers wearing monster costumes, and photographed in miniature sets, as in GODZILLA, KING OF THE MONSTERS (1956) and GORGO (1960).

THE LOST WORLD (1960): A magnified lizard poses smugly under the klieg lights.

4) <u>Mechanical mock-ups</u>. Miniature or life-sized constructions, built for live-action filming, as in THE LAND UNKNOWN (1957) and THE MONSTER THAT CHALLENGED THE WORLD (1957).

Each of these four methods has advantages and disadvantages, and each can be used successfully according to individual script requirements and the degree of care involved in their application; each technique has produced examples of sterling craftsmanship as well as dismal failures, a scale ranging from the heights of KING KONG (1933) to the ignominious depths of THE GIANT CLAW (1957).

Although there are many regrettable and even unintentionally amusing examples of inept special effects perpetrated by uncaring or unfortunately poverty-stricken technicians, in most cases the efforts of those responsible for the effects in these pictures are commendable, allowing for the difficulties imposed by limited budgets and rushed shooting schedules. Even if the final results are at times less than convincing, the inevitable classification of these films as trivial entertainments should not detract from the credit due the many dedicated craftsmen involved in their production.

Although there have been many notable animated cartoon forays into the realm of prehistory, as in Walt Disney's classic FANTASIA (1940), the live-action representation of prehistoric monsters has always been more impressive and infinitely more difficult to achieve convincingly onscreen.

This book presents the best of the live-action "prehistoric" monster movies, covering every noteworthy theatrical feature-length film, along with comparative lesser examples, complete with cast and production credit listings, photos, and, wherever possible, comments and information provided by those individuals responsible for their production. Prehistory is often used as a tenuous explanation for giantism in fictional monsters that never really existed. Many of these are included here, but artifically created monstrosities, such as the giant ants in THEM (1954), are excluded. Like most of the movies examined, this volume seeks to entertain, with a little worthwhile technical and historical information offered in the bargain.

1. SILENT PREHISTORY

The silent film, stylized by necessity as much as by design, readily embraced fantasy, and audiences accepted such movies with enthusiasm. Silent fantasies like THE THIEF OF BAGDAD (1924) possess a mystical, fairy-tale quality that is difficult to achieve with sound; the silents, because they demanded viewer concentration by their very nature, drew their audience into them and achieved maximum effectiveness as a result.

Early fantasy movies embracing a "prehistoric" theme did not seek to convince as much as simply exploit viewer interest in the subject; at this time evolution was still controversial, and most "prehistoric" fantasies were either light farces or brief morality plays. Renowned director D.W. Griffith filmed MAN'S GENESIS in 1912 for Biograph; this ten-minute drama featured Robert Harron and Mae Marsh as primitive cave dwellers. It was successful enough to warrant a 20-minute sequel, THE PRIMITIVE MAN (1913), also known under the alternate titles BRUTE FORCE and WARS OF PRIMAL TRIBES. The first half of THE PRIMITIVE MAN simply reused all the footage from MAN'S GENESIS, which had contained no prehistoric animals, but the second reel of THE PRIMITIVE MAN exhibited what may be the screen's first dinosaurs--stiff, mechanical, life-sized mock-ups and enlarged reptiles. This was unintentionally prophetic since Griffith, at the end of his career, would direct at least part of ONE MILLION B.C. (1940).

In 1914, comedian Charlie Chaplin stumbled across the stone-age terrain in HIS PREHISTORIC PAST, a ten-minute comedy released by Keystone, but Chaplin's Little Tramp encountered no dinosaurs in the film, nor did the casts of such other early "prehistoric" silents as THE CAVEMAN (Vitagraph,

THE DINOSAUR AND THE MISSING LINK: This early Willis
O'Brien creation shows similarities to the later KING KONG
(frame enlargement).

1912) and THE SERPENTS, another 1912 Vitagraph release
using footage from THE CAVEMAN.

It wasn't until the emergence of a remarkable film craftsman named Willis Harold O'Brien that the first convincing prehistoric monsters appeared on film. Born in 1886, there was
little about O'Brien's early life to suggest his eventual stature
in the motion picture industry. Rather aimless in his youth,
O'Brien led a varied, roustabout existence, wandering from
rodeos to employment as a train brakeman, and was an assistant sculptor at the 1913 San Francisco World's Fair.

It was around this time that O'Brien first began to ex-
periment with stop-motion animation. Although he did not

invent the process, he apparently discovered it independently
of any other influence. Animating the clay figure of a boxer
as a lark, O'Brien was intrigued by the technique, and he
shot a brief test reel as a demonstration of the process. When
Herman Wobber, a film exhibitor, saw this reel in 1915, he
was so impressed that he offered O'Brien $5,000 to animate
a five-minute film, THE DINOSAUR AND THE MISSING LINK,
which was so successful it was later reissued as THE DINO-
SAUR AND THE BABOON. The little picture was released
by Thomas Edison's film company in 1917, and O'Brien was
immediately offered employment at Edison's New York studios
to produce a series of similar animated movies. As the dili-
gent O'Brien progressed with his first crude efforts, he could
not have known that his endeavors would shape the rest of
his life and eventually result in one of the greatest films
ever made.

    Each of the Edison releases ran 200 to 500 feet in length,
and O'Brien was paid $1 per finished foot of film. From the
beginning, O'Brien was interested in prehistoric subjects;
other titles in this series, which Edison released under the
Conquest Films banner, were MORPHEUS MIKE and THE BIRTH
OF A FLIVVER (these two were shot outside the Edison studios, before Edison acquired THE DINOSAUR AND THE MISS-
ING LINK for distribution), 10,000 YEARS B.C. (1917), also
known as 2,000,000 B.C. and GFD 10,000 B.C. (this was the
first O'Brien short actually produced for Edison), PREHIS-
TORIC POULTRY (1917), CURIOUS PETS OF OUR ANCESTORS
(1917), THE PUZZLING BILLBOARD (for a proposed series,
SAM LLOYD'S PICTURE PUZZLES), and a series of one-reelers
titled MICKEY'S NAUGHTY NIGHTMARES, which featured a
live boy combined with cartoon animation.

    These short films were meant to be nothing more than
brief diversions shown between features since they were
charming and amusing. But the Edison studios were sinking
financially. O'Brien left the company in 1917 and met sculptor
Herbert M. Dawley, who was interested in the reconstruction
of prehistoric animals. Dawley had constructed several large
inanimate mock-ups of dinosaurs himself, and, impressed by
O'Brien's work, advanced the animator $3,000 to film THE
GHOST OF SLUMBER MOUNTAIN from his own story. The
ten-minute film required three months shooting time. The
plot concerns a mountain climber who dreams that he has met
the ghost of a hermit; this spirit possesses a magical telescope

PREHISTORIC POULTRY: A quizzical dinornis (frame enlargement).

which reveals life on earth as it existed millions of years ago. O'Brien animated several dinosaurs for the prehistoric scenes, his work exhibiting more detail and realism that his previous efforts. When it was released by the World Film Corporation in 1919, THE GHOST OF SLUMBER MOUNTAIN was a considerable financial success, returning $100,000 in profits on the original $3,000 investment. O'Brien's dinosaur footage from THE GHOST OF SLUMBER MOUNTAIN also appeared in another Dawley short, ALONG THE MOONBEAM TRAIL (1920), as well as the Max Fleischer feature EVOLUTION, released by Red Seal pictures in 1923.

Watterson R. Rothacker, a former Chicago journalist who produced OLD DOC YAK, one of the first important animated cartoon films, saw enormous potential in O'Brien's animation and obtained film rights to Sir Arthur Conan Doyle's fantasy-adventure novel THE LOST WORLD. After joining forces with First National studios, he and O'Brien filmed what would ultimately become one of the most influential and successful pictures of its type ever made.

2. THE LOST WORLD

First National, 1925

Credits:

Producers: Watterson R. Rothacker and Earl Hudson
Director: Harry O. Hoyt
Screenplay: Marion Fairfax; based on the novel by Sir Arthur Conan Doyle
Camera: Arthur Edeson
Special Effects: Willis O'Brien
Technical Staff: Fred W. Jackman, Ralph Hammeras, Marcel Delgado, Homer Scott, J. Devereaux Jennings, and Vernon L. Walker
Set Design: Milton Menasco
Editor: George McGuire
Assistant Director: William Dowling

Cast:

Bessie Love (Paula White)
Lloyd Hughes (Edward J. Malone)
Lewis Stone (Sir John Roxton)
Wallace Beery (Prof. Challenger)
Arthur Hoyt (Prof. Summerlee)
Margaret McWade (Mrs. Challenger)
Finch Smiles (Austin)
Jules Cowles (Zambo)
Bull Montana (ape-man)
George Bunny (Colin McArdle)
Charles Wellesley (Maj. Hibbard)
Alma Bennett (Gladys Hungerford)
Virginia Browne Faire (half-caste girl)
Nelson MacDowell (attorney)

THE LOST WORLD: Wallace Beery, Lewis Stone, Bessie Love,
and Lloyd Hughes plan their expedition.

     With Earl J. Hudson as production supervisor, filming
on THE LOST WORLD began in 1923 at First National studios.
Marcel Delgado, a young art student who would assist O'Brien
on several films, was employed to construct the miniature
dinosaurs for the picture, about fifty of them altogether.
Built up with red sponge rubber over fully jointed metal armatures with meticulously detailed outer skins, O'Brien's monsters for THE LOST WORLD exhibited a degree of sophisti-
cation far in advance of his previous work. Not only were
the models larger than before, allowing greater textural detail, but some of them were even outfitted with internal air
bladders, which allowed them to "breathe" during animation,
as air was pumped in and withdrawn by increments during
the frame-by-frame photography. At 16 frames per second
at the silent film speed, every minute of projected monster
action required 960 separate exposures. A ten-hour workday
yielding 35 feet of completed animation footage, or 20 seconds
of screen time, was considered productive. Not surprisingly,
the picture took over 14 months to film in an era of depart-

mentalized studio production when the average feature film
was shot in less than a month.

Based on Sir Arthur Conan Doyle's fantasy-adventure
novel, the film relates the story of an expedition, led by
Professor Challenger, to a South American plateau in search
of a missing explorer. Prehistoric animals still live atop the
plateau, and the party captures an injured brontosaurus.
Returning to civilization with the monster as proof of their
adventure, the huge beast escapes, destructively roaming
through the streets of London before collapsing London
Bridge under its weight and swimming away, presumably to
return home, at the fade out.

Before offering any evaluation of THE LOST WORLD as
a film, it must be explained that any such opinion is neces-
sarily compromised by the fact that the complete film as it
was released in 1925 no longer exists. Originally 108 minutes

THE LOST WORLD: Bessie Love cringes before an inquisitive
brontosaurus.

in length, current prints of THE LOST WORLD run only about
60 minutes; these prints are, in fact, dupes of the 16mm
abridged home movie version, prepared by the Kodascope
company for film hobbyists and school use years ago. The
script of the original version does exist, however, revealing
an entire sub-plot involving Lloyd Hughes and his fiancée,
which is only mentioned briefly in the Kodascope abridge-
ment, and at least another reel of footage was expended at a
South American trading post, where a half-caste girl caused
problems for the expedition. These portions would appear
to be mostly padding leading up to the exciting monster sequences on the plateau, but such a judgment is tenuous without the actual scenes on hand for critical evaluation.

Fortunately, most of the O'Brien monster animation remains intact, although specific shots (such as the brontosaurus destroying a London club and mauling the occupants)
were deleted as being too explicit for the school trade, which
accounted for a large portion of the 16mm market at that
time. The complete original version of THE LOST WORLD
may well be gone forever; the original negative no longer
exists. In 1948 the negative was turned over to Encyclopaedia Britannica, Inc., which edited a ten-minute film called
A LOST WORLD from the original material, and apparently
the negative, on nitrate stock as most films of that time were,
deteriorated and was junked while in the company's posses-
sion. No known film archive has a complete print. The only
longer print, an original Kodascope copy padded with about
five extra minutes of clips, some of which appear to have
been duped from 9.5mm and some of which were apparently
reduced from 35mm footage--although not many animation
scenes were included in these extra shots--was screened at
the Cinémathèque in Belgium about 20 years ago.

Duplicate picture elements were never found in the
Warner Bros.-First National vaults. The only hope for future
recovery would depend upon a complete nitrate release print
turning up, which, although possible, seems highly unlikely
at this late date, especially since First National always en-
forced meticulous accounting of all their prints, and few of
them ever circulate among private collectors. Not only is
THE LOST WORLD now severely abridged, but the prints
now available are merely duplicates of the Kodascope abridge-
ment, so the film's visual quality, important to its success,
especially in the animation scenes, has been impaired as well.

THE LOST WORLD: The explorers watch a family of animated triceratops.

The Encyclopaedia Britannica one-reeler, prints of which still circulate, has much greater picture clarity since it was printed from the original negative. It is a depressing reminder of how degraded the current prints of THE LOST WORLD are.

This said, the film is still entertaining, even in its present form. Wallace Beery would seem to be an odd choice for the role of a professor, but he conforms perfectly to Doyle's written description of the burly Challenger, which is quite enough for a silent film, where Beery's gruff voice is not a drawback. Pretty Bessie Love is charming and vivacious as the daughter of the explorer sought by the expedition, and Lewis Stone lends solid support as Sir John Roxton, who finances the expedition, with Lloyd Hughes offering a dependable hero and Bull Montana stealing scenes at intervals as a furry, snarling prehistoric ape man.

O'Brien's animation is impressive; the movements of the

THE LOST WORLD: A pair of trachodons, crudely detailed
since they were not prominently featured in the film.

monsters are generally smooth and the miniature sets, built
by Ralph Hammeras and his crew, are detailed beyond anything seen prior to this film, with backdrops consisting of
photo blow-ups or paintings. The lively monsters exhibit almost human qualities on occasion, with their grimacing faces
and rolling eyes; O'Brien was a cartoonist at one time, and
it shows in his work, which is vigorous and entertaining.
One scene, shot on a vast 75- by 150-foot miniature landscape set, in which the dinosaurs stampede as they flee an
erupting volcano, is an impressive display of technical virtuosity, as dozens of the animated monsters scurry about
simultaneously in the same shot.

Since optical printers were not used at this time, the
scenes in THE LOST WORLD combining the live performers
with the monsters were achieved in the camera using split-
screen stationary mattes. A typical shot would depict Wallace
Beery and his companions in the lower left corner of the
screen as they observe an animated brontosaurus in the center of the frame. This was filmed by shooting the actors
through a sheet of glass as they cowered, for instance,
against a tree. The entire glass area on the opposite side
of the tree was opaqued with black paint or tape so that
this area of the film remained unexposed. The acting of
Beery and friends completed, the footage was rewound to
the beginning and delivered to O'Brien, who animated his
dinosaur on the same film while shooting through a counter-
matte, thus achieving a perfect blending of the two separately
filmed images. On some shots a third step was necessary to
superimpose additional details, such as smoke or fog.

The Williams traveling matte process, invented by
Frank D. Williams in 1916, is used with varying degrees of
success in the scenes showing the brontosaurus in London.
The process suffered from technical crudities at the time,
though, and in some shots a telltale fringe is clearly visible
around the monster. A huge prop tail and foot were also
used in these scenes for direct interaction with the terrorized
crowds.

THE LOST WORLD was a huge success when first released and would ultimately prove to be one of the most influential fantasy pictures ever made. By contrast, the 1960
remake of THE LOST WORLD was an innocuous and instantly
forgotten mediocrity. Produced by Irwin Allen, magnified

<u>Above</u>: THE LOST WORLD (1925): An allosaurus attacks
the brontosaurus.
<u>Below</u>: THE LOST WORLD (1960); In the inferior remake,
magnified reptiles were used instead of stop-motion animation,
with variable results, as this frame enlargement demonstrates
(photo courtesy of George Turner.)

lizards were used instead of stop-motion animation, despite
the fact that, just a few years before, Allen had produced
THE ANIMAL WORLD (1956), which offered dinosaurs animated
by Willis O'Brien and Ray Harryhausen, and O'Brien was employed in a supervisory capacity on Allen's remake of THE
LOST WORLD.

That O'Brien was not allowed to duplicate his effects
of 35 years earlier is a tragedy; the remake's special effects
succeed well enough in individual shots, but are used too infrequently to be effective. When a miscast Claude Rains
(who has the bluster but certainly not the physical stature
for the role of Challenger) sees an enlarged lizard and exclaims "A brontosaurus!" with a straight face, all credibility
is lost. Despite the remake's sound, color and Cinemascope,
the 1925 silent original remains far superior.

After THE LOST WORLD, two other Willis O'Brien projects for First National were cancelled: a film based on the
story of the legendary sunken city of Atlantis and a proposed
version of FRANKENSTEIN, in which the monster was to have
been animated by O'Brien. It was while he was shooting test
scenes at RKO studios for another cancelled production, a
prehistoric adventure to be called CREATION, that O'Brien's
stop-motion animation caught the attention of producer Merian
C. Cooper, who had been considering filming a fantastic adventure story about a giant gorilla.

3. KING KONG

RKO, 1933

Credits:

Executive Producer: David O. Selznick
Producers: Merian C. Cooper and Ernest B. Schoedsack
Directors: Merian C. Cooper and Ernest B. Schoedsack
Screenplay: James Creelman and Ruth Rose; from an idea
   conceived by Merian C. Cooper and Edgar Wallace
Camera: Eddie Linden, Vernon Walker, and J.O. Taylor
Special Effects: Willis O'Brien
Art Technicians: Mario Larrinaga and Byron L. Crabbe
Technical Staff: E.B. Gibson, Marcel Delgado, Fred Reefe,
   Orville Goldner, and Carroll Shepphird
Sets: Carroll Clark and Al Herman
Music: Max Steiner
Sound: Murray Spivack and Earl A. Wolcott
Editor: Ted Cheesman
Production Assistants: Archie F. Marshek and Walter Daniels

Cast:

Fay Wray (Ann Darrow)
Robert Armstrong (Carl Denham)
Bruce Cabot (Jack Driscoll)
Frank Reicher (Captain Englehorn)
Sam Hardy (Weston)
Noble Johnson (native chief)
Steve Clemente (witch king)
James Flavin (first mate)
Victor Wong (Charlie)

Few movies have been able to match the longevity and
continuing popularity of the original KING KONG, the best
fantasy adventure film ever made.   More than a great fantasy
picture, KING KONG trancends its own genre and stands as
one of the greatest movies of any type ever produced.   Even
the highly publicized, grossly over-budgeted (and disastrously
inept) 1976 remake has not dimmed the original's appeal.

With this film Willis O'Brien's stop-motion animation effects blossomed into full flower.   Basing his visual design on
the eerie black and white drawings of Gustav Dore, O'Brien's
crew brought forth an alien, strangely beautiful prehistoric
landscape on the lost island inhabited by Kong, the huge ape
and prehistoric monsters animated with a degree of vitality
unattained before and seldom achieved since.   Incredibly,
only eight years separate THE LOST WORLD from KING KONG.
Without criticizing THE LOST WORLD, the two films seem
light years apart technically.   Constructed on a huge scale
(the brontosaurus model alone was several feet in length)
these beautifully crafted animation models, built by Marcel
Delgado, possess great textural detail, their large size allowing subtlety and maximum flexibility in lighting.   The cameras
could move in quite close without destroying the illusion of
size.   (The desiccated remnants of these monster models survive today, on display in the science-fiction museum of Forrest J Ackerman in Los Angeles.)

KING KONG was the brainchild of producer Merian C.
Cooper, who co-directed with his long-time partner Ernest
B. Schoedsack (together they had filmed the great documen-
taries GRASS and CHANG, as well as THE FOUR FEATHERS)
under executive producer David O. Selznick's protective
supervision (even though Selznick's creative imput was almost
nil, he effectively prevented executive interference with the
production, allowing Cooper and Schoedsack to make the film
exactly the way they wanted to).   The picture was in production for over a year, costing $678,000 (at a time when the
average studio film was budgeted at $200,000), but it proved
immediately beneficial to financially troubled RKO on release;
the film grossed nearly $2,000,000 for the studio in the dark-
est days of the Great Depression, becoming one of the high-
est grossing movies of the thirties.   Reissued six times by
RKO (with the 1952 rerelease proving especially successful,
earning nearly $3,000,000), and reissued again by Janus
Films on a limited basis in the early 1970s, the picture continues to demonstrate its popularity through highly rated

KING KONG: A posed publicity shot of Robert Armstrong and Fay Wray, in costume for the Skull Island scenes.

television showings and videocassette sales.

By this point in time, few can be unfamiliar with the plot of KING KONG, but a synopsis is presented here as a framework supporting a detailed examination of this landmark film's influential special effects.

Carl Denham, a noted documentary filmmaker (written by Ruth Rose--Mrs. Ernest Schoedsack--as a gentle satire of Merian C. Cooper), is seeking a leading lady for his next production, his distributors having informed him that he must include romantic interest in his adventure films to insure box-office success. Denham must find his star soon, though; he is due to leave on his filmmaking expedition the following morning and all the theatrical agencies, aware of his notorious reputation for recklessness, have refused to provide an actress.

Denham searches for a leading lady himself in Manhattan and eventually discovers Ann Darrow, a beautiful unemployed film extra. (This scene was based on a true incident; when Steve Clemente, who plays the witch doctor in the film, once needed an assistant for his knife-throwing act, he embarked on a similar mission through the city streets until he discovered an attractive candidate for the job.) Denham takes the down-and-out Ann to dinner and offers her the lead in his picture, which she accepts with trepidation. Setting sail the next morning on board The Venture, Ann meets Jack Driscoll, the freighter's gruff first mate. Until the voyage, Denham has been secretive about the exact destination of the expedition, refusing to reveal the details even to the captain and the first mate until they reach the South Pacific. At that point Denham reveals an ominous map sold to him by a Norwegian captain, which indicates a remote uncharted island with a huge wall dividing the interior jungle from the beach area. Setting their course for Skull Island (so named because the dome of a prominent mountain there resembles a human skull in form), they approach at night (there is a wonderfully atmospheric shot of The Venture enshrouded in fog, represented by a meticulously detailed model only a few feet in length). The threatening sound of native drums are heard in the distance. As they prepare to land in a lifeboat the

---

[Opposite:] KING KONG: The hapless sailors about to meet their end. The styracosaurus at right was cut from the sequence in order to tighten the editing.

next day, O'Brien's first animated monsters are seen in the form of birds, or perhaps flying reptiles, careening above the island like harbingers of doom. Arriving on the beach, Denham and his party interrupt a native ceremony in which a girl is being sacrificed to the god Kong, and the natives become excited when they see Ann, offering to buy her from Denham as a sacrifice for their god. Fearing for the girl's safety, Denham and his companions retreat to the ship; that night, Ann and Jack admit their love for each other, but when she is alone Ann is kidnapped by the natives, who have approached the ship unseen in a canoe.

The terrified Ann is brought to the native village, where she is prepared for sacrifice to Kong in a frenzied ceremony. Ann is bound to a sacrificial altar beyond the huge gates leading through the wall, and the fearsome Kong, summoned by a native gong, appears to claim his prize. The huge ape is about 20 feet tall. (The often quoted height of 50 feet is false, the product of an over-zealous RKO publicity department. O'Brien scaled the ape to appear 18 feet tall in the jungle scenes and 24 feet tall in the later city scenes; the size was kept flexible to insure maximum visual impact from scene to scene, depending on the surroundings.) Kong plucks the screaming Ann from the altar and carries her into the jungle. (In the scene showing Kong's approach to the altar the 18-inch tall animated Kong is in the background and the full-scale altar with Fay Wray, in front of a full-scale pair of trees, timed to fall aside in synchronization with the miniature Kong's hand and arm movements as he apparently pushes them apart, are all matted onto the background action of the miniature ape. As Kong picks up Ann, she falls from the altar and is momentarily out of view behind the altar as an animated figure is substituted for the real actress to allow interaction as the animated Kong picks her up. When Ann is next seen in Kong's grasp, she is an animated figure.)

Discovering Ann's abduction, Denham, Driscoll, and the Venture crew storm the island, just in time to see Kong disappear into the jungle with Ann in his grasp (these incredibly detailed miniature jungle sets were created by Orville Goldner). Forcing the huge gates open, they pursue the ape and are confronted by a stegosaurus (an animated model enlarged via rear projection behind the actors). Killing the charging dinosaur with a barrage of rifle fire, they edge past the huge carcass as the spiked tail undulates in

KING KONG: The dynamic tyrannosaurus battle.   Fay Wray
watches from the safety of a tree.

spasmodic death throes (in this shot the actors are walking
on an off-screen treadmill, timed in synchronization with the
rear-projected dinosaur footage, creating the illusion that
they are walking past the monster).

Continuing through the jungle, Denham and his men
hastily construct a raft in order to cross a swamp, but are
capsized by a brontosaurus (this scene uses a live-action
model of the dinosaur--the surrounding water prohibiting
animation--overturning a miniature raft and sailors; one shot
of the live-action sailors just before the raft is overturned
is matted onto background footage of the miniature brontosaurus approaching the raft).   After killing a number of the

sailors, the enraged dinosaur pursues Denham, Driscoll and
the remaining members of the rescue party into the jungle;
fleeing, they attempt to cross a log bridging a gorge. Kong,
having placed the unconscious Ann in the safety of a tree,
arrives and begins to shake the men from the log just as
Denham and Driscoll reach safety on opposite sides of the
gorge (this scene is realized with the full-scale prop log and
sailors matted onto the footage of the miniature Kong, with
the movements of the ape and log synchronized so that Kong
appears to be holding it). In a rage, Kong hurls the log
into the ravine, with one sailor still desperately clinging to
it. (Originally, this scene was to have included an animated
styracosaurus, which prevented the sailors from escaping
Kong by simply running off the log in the other direction,
as well as a grisly scene in the pit below showing animated
giant insects and lizards devouring the sailors. This material
was excised before release in order to tighten the editing;
these shots never appeared in any release print of the film.)

Driscoll has taken refuge in a small cave in the ravine
wall just below Kong and is nearly attacked by a lizard creep-
ing up the vine towards him, but he cuts the vine with his
knife and the lizard falls into the pit below. Kong, suddenly
noticing Driscoll, lunges at the sailor, but Driscoll slashes
the ape's groping paw with his knife, and Kong withdraws to
nurse his wounds. (This is one of the most technically complicated scenes in the picture, using a miniature rear-projection
system invented by O'Brien as a means of introducing live-
action elements into miniature sets. In the long shots of this
scene, as Kong reaches for Bruce Cabot in the cave, the live-
action footage of the cowering actor is projected from behind
the set onto a small translucent screen in the cave opening,
one frame at a time, as the ape is animated in reaction to
Cabot's footage. When the animated lizard creeps upward on
the vine, Cabot attracts Kong's attention by cutting the reptile loose, and the camera pans upward to catch Kong's reaction. This introduces yet another animation element, as the
camera itself must be animated upwards in precise increments
in order to execute a pan while the ape and live-action footage are taken progressively through their frame-by-frame
movements.)

Meanwhile, a hungry tyrannosaurus has approached
Ann, still reclining in the treetop where Kong had placed
her. The girl's screams draw Kong away from Driscoll, and

KING KONG: The tyrannosaurus in a heavily detailed miniature set.   Note how the foreground jungle foliage, painted
on glass, adds depth to the scene (frame enlargement).

the huge ape savagely battles the dinosaur until it dies.
(When the animated monsters first begin their confrontation
in this thrilling sequence, rear-projection is used as Miss
Wray observes the monsters from her vantage point in the
foreground tree, with an animated figure substituted for the
actress in a couple of the long shots.)   The tree containing
Ann is felled as the beasts clash, pinning the otherwise un-
harmed Ann beneath it as the battle continues.   (A live-action
Fay Wray observes the monsters from beside the tree, the
actress incorporated into the scene via the Dunning matte
process.   The matte photography in KING KONG uses two
different matte processes: the aforementioned Dunning process and the newly improved Williams matte process, which
was made available to the production midway through shooting.   The remainder of the picture employed the superior
Williams process, which allowed greater flexibility in the optical printing stage when the separate picture elements were

combined.) Grasping Ann, the victorious Kong arrives at a
subterranean grotto leading to his mountaintop lair, with a
stealthy Driscoll in hidden pursuit as Denham hurries to rejoin the Venture crew waiting at the huge wall in a plan to
return with reinforcements.

Within Kong's grotto, the ape momentarily places Ann
on a ledge as a cautious Driscoll watches from behind a concealing boulder, hoping for an opportunity to rescue Ann.
Suddenly, an elasmosaurus attacks the girl, and Kong grap-
ples with the monster, killing it. (In this scene live-action
elements of Fay Wray and Bruce Cabot are introduced via
miniature rear-projection as the animated monsters fight, with
the further detail of volcanic steam, rising upwards, added
via superimposition.) The ape carries Ann along a narrow
rocky path and through a cave opening leading to a preci-
pice high atop Skull Mountain. Curious about the girl, Kong
removes some of her clothing, inspecting his prize, but is
interrupted when Driscoll, close on the ape's trail, clumsily
overturns a boulder in the cave. Kong leaves Ann to investigate the noise, and while he is gone a hungry pterodactyl
attacks Ann, but Kong, alerted by her screams, kills the flying reptile after a brief struggle. While Kong is distracted,
Driscoll reaches Ann, and the couple attempt an escape by
climbing down a long vine growing on the cliff. Suddenly,
Kong sees them, and when he begins pulling the vine back
towards him, Ann and Jack leap from it, plunging safely into
the river far below.

(The scene in which Kong plucks at Fay Wray's clothing is one of the most convincing in the film, with the actress cradled in a full-scale hand and arm, blended with the
animated miniature via rear projection. Bits of clothing were
removed from the actress with invisible wires, and the miniature Kong's hand movements were animated to correspond with
this action in the background film, with actual bits of cloth
substituted in the puppet's hand at appropriate intervals.
It should be noted that this scene never exceeds the bounds
of decency, even at the conclusion of the episode; Miss Wray
remains clothed to a degree, despite her monstrous captor's
inquisitive nature. The Kong-pterodactyl battle was a complicated scene requiring seven weeks of animation time, with
the model of the flying reptile suspended in mid-air during
animation as live-action footage of Fay Wray and Bruce Cabot
was added via miniature rear-projection, with the performers

replaced with animated figures at certain points in the scene.
During this sequence, there is a bit of subliminal detail added
as the animated sun in the afternoon sky slowly sets through
a cloud bank, the diffused rays emerging from the under-
side of the cloud. This takes place behind the action and is
not the focal point of attention; intricate detail like this is a
hallmark of O'Brien's work.)

Fleeing through the jungle, Ann and Jack rejoin Denham and the crew at the gates, but Kong follows them, the
enraged beast crashing through the gates and destroying the
native village before Denham subdues the monster with a well-
placed gas bomb. (The shots of Kong rampaging through
the village and mauling the natives employ animated figures
of the natives when Kong interacts with them, in addition to
live-action elements blended with the animated puppet via
rear-projection and matte photography. One scene, in which
Kong destroys a native hut, is cleverly achieved by animating Kong uprooting a miniature hut, tossing it upward out
of frame, and then substituting full-scale wreckage, dropped
from above in the foreground in front of this rear-projected
scene. This trick set-up is repeated later in the city scenes,
with the debris of a building damaged by Kong.)

Realizing the potential in exploiting the monster, Denham abandons his film-making plans and transports the ape
back to New York, placing the chained beast on display before an opening night theatre crowd, with Ann and Jack
present. As newspaper photographers snap photos of Kong,
the monster is enraged by their flashbulbs, thinking that
they are harming Ann. Suddenly breaking free, Kong
crashes through the theatre wall as Ann and Jack flee to
the safety of a nearby hotel, and the huge ape roams through
the city streets, destroying property and killing several people
as he searches for her. As Driscoll comforts a distraught
Ann, Kong scales the building outside, and seeing the girl
through a window, reaches in and recaptures her, brushing
Driscoll aside. Rampaging through the streets with his re-
claimed prize, Kong destroys an elevated train, killing many
of the passengers. (The scenes of Kong in the streets of
New York were achieved in much the same manner as his
destruction of the native village; live-action crowds are introduced into the shots via rear-projection and mattes. Kong's
appearance at the window as he searches for Ann is full-
scale rear-projection, and the monster's spectacular destruction

of the elevated train is convincingly detailed as live-action
spectators are added to the scene via matte photography. A
point-of-view shot of Kong leering at the train as it approaches
was filmed by mounting the camera on the scale-model tracks
and moving it forward by increments as the ape was animated
frame-by-frame. Interestingly, this effective scene was a
last-minute afterthought, and the train sequence was conceived after shooting had already been wrapped, with the
film going back into production for this one scene.)

Scaling the Empire State Building with his captive, Kong
battles army planes armed with submachine guns, eventually
falling to his death in the street below, as Jack Driscoll
rushes to the pinnacle of the building and is reunited with
Ann Darrow. (The dynamic conclusion atop the Empire State
Building was filmed with the animated Kong astride a miniature building; for the distant view of Kong scaling the edi-
fice) the animated figure was matted onto a long shot of the
actual structure, with a cringing Fay Wray introduced with
rear-projection. When Kong picks her up briefly, the actress is replaced by an animated figure. The attacking planes
are animated in many shots, in other views, footage of real
planes photographed in New York is used. The point-of-
view shots of the planes diving at Kong were achieved by
moving the camera forward by increments as the ape was
animated, as in the train scene. The two pilots shown in
close-up are played by Cooper and Schoedsack. The city
backdrop is an intricately detailed glass painting.)

Some full-scale props were used to represent Kong; a
huge life-sized mechanical head (used throughout the film
for close-ups and for grisly scenes in which Kong chews his
victims in the native village and New York). A mechanical
hand and arm for grasping Fay Wray was used in several
shots, as well as a huge prop foot, which ground several
natives beneath its heel. Nowhere in the film was the ape
ever portrayed by an actor in a costume, as has sometimes
been erroneously reported.

Glass paintings, mostly of jungle foliage, are used
throughout the film to lend an illusion of depth to the miniature sets; the animated models are often sandwiched between
several sheets of lavishly rendered glass artwork, with subliminal animation adding even further detail in the form of
birds flittering through the dense jungle. Through this

impressive array of technical ingenuity, a fictional prehistoric
ape and the frightening saurian denizens of Skull Island were
brought to thrilling and convincing life.

The acting in KING KONG is intentionally styled larger
than life in order to impart a mythic, timeless stature to the
film. (Cecil B. De Mille used the same technique as late as
1956 in his Vistavision epic THE TEN COMMANDMENTS.) The
KING KONG cast is one of the most enjoyable ever to grace
a fantasy picture. Robert Armstrong was cast as Carl Denham after Cooper saw him in a ZaSu Pitts comedy. Bruce
Cabot, who was new to films, won the role of Driscoll after
Joel McCrea turned it down.

Although Fay Wray is remembered today mainly for her
performances in KING KONG and four other classic 1930s
thrillers (DOCTOR X, THE MOST DANGEROUS GAME, MYS-
TERY OF THE WAX MUSEUM and THE VAMPIRE BAT), her
career encompassed much more than those memorable appearances as a terrified heroine. She did not perform exclusively
in the horror genre, and only five of the impressive total of
77 features she was seen in from 1925 to 1958 (67 of them as
a leading lady) can be classified as horror.

Indeed, the extent of Fay Wray's career may come as
somewhat of a surprise to many. A likeable, dependable, and
competent actress, she has been directed by talents as diverse as William A. Wellman, Mauritz Stiller, Erich von Stroheim, Alan Crosland, Frank Capra, Raoul Walsh, Michael Cur-
tiz, Jack Conway, Karl Freund, Roy William Neill, and Josef
von Sternberg. Her leading men have included Gary Cooper,
Emil Jannings, William Powell, Richard Arlen, Clark Gable,
Jack Holt, Spencer Tracy, Ralph Bellamy, Fredric March, Wallace Beery, Joel McCrea, and Claude Rains.

Fay Wray (her real name) was born in Alberta, Canada
on September 10, 1907, on her father's farm. Her family
moved to Los Angeles while she was very young, and after
appearing in a few high school plays Fay began working in
movies at the age of 16 in 1923. She did comedy shorts for
Hal Roach, and in 1925 made her feature film debut in THE
COAST PATROL, a low-budget independent production. This
was followed by a contract with Universal Pictures which
placed her in a series of westerns with such leading men as
Art Acord, Jack Hoxie, and Hoot Gibson. It looked as though

her career wouldn't advance beyond this point when she
landed the starring role in Erich von Stroheim's lavish production of THE WEDDING MARCH. Only 19 at the time, her performance as Mitzi in this tale of the ill-fated romance between
an aristocrat and a commoner in old Vienna was exceptional,
and some of her scenes were quite touching. THE WEDDING
MARCH is arguably von Stroheim's best picture. Fay Wray's
showcase role should have made her a major star and probably would have if the film hadn't taken so long to produce.
By the time Paramount released the film in 1928, sound had
already captured the public's interest and THE WEDDING
MARCH did not receive very wide distribution. Despite generally favorable reviews, relatively few people saw the picture.
Filmed in two parts, the second half, THE HONEYMOON, was
never released in this country due to von Stroheim's objections over the editing of the film.

Wray did win a Paramount contract as a result of THE
WEDDING MARCH. Although most of the pictures she appeared
in at that studio were innocuous and generally forgettable,
there were a few noteworthy exceptions. Besides appearing
in DIRIGIBLE for Frank Capra, she turned in a good performance for Josef von Sternberg in THUNDERBOLT. Her
brief role in THE FOUR FEATHERS introduced her to the
producer-director team of Merian C. Cooper and Ernest B.
Schoedsack, who would later have bigger things in store for
her with KING KONG.

In 1928, Fay met writer John Monk Saunders (WINGS)
on the set of LEGION OF THE CONDEMNED, in which she
starred with Gary Cooper. She and Saunders were married
later that same year. Decision-makers at Paramount tried
several times to pair her with Gary Cooper in a series of
films, only to be met with lukewarm box office response. She
was released from her Paramount contract in 1931 and free-
lanced. DOCTOR X, released in late 1932, was the first of
Fay's horror roles, and she looked especially attractive in
the film's duo-tone Technicolor. DOCTOR X was followed by
THE MOST DANGEROUS GAME at RKO. The suspense thriller
was directed by Ernest B. Schoedsack (with Irving Pichel)
and produced by Merian C. Cooper, who was also preparing

[Opposite:] KING KONG: Kong rescues Fay Wray from a
pterodactyl in a scene that took several weeks to animate.

the film that would ultimately become KING KONG. Fay and
her MOST DANGEROUS GAME co-star Robert Armstrong were
assigned the leads, and the rest is film history. KING KONG
gave Fay first billing, but, paradoxically, the movie's great
success had little effect on the course of her career.

KING KONG did not typecast Fay Wray in horror films
as is commonly believed. DOCTOR X, THE MOST DANGEROUS
GAME and MYSTERY OF THE WAX MUSEUM (her other Technicolor horror outing) were all released before KING KONG;
only THE VAMPIRE BAT was released afterwards. Appearing in a total of 11 feature in 1933, Fay continued to work
steadily at the major studios (she was in the prestigious
VIVA VILLA at M-G-M in 1934) until she traveled to England
to perform in a quartet of features in 1935. Upon her return to Hollywood the next year, her career had lost momentum, and although there was no shortage of roles for her,
from this point on she appeared almost exclusively in "B"
pictures. Her nonexclusive contract with Columbia specified
four movies a year and granted her the right to free-lance;
she did films at RKO, Universal and Monogram, few of which
were noteworthy. In 1939 she and John Monk Saunders,
whose personal problems, particularly with alcohol, had grown
insurmountable, were divorced shortly after the birth of their
daughter Susan. Saunders died shortly thereafter. Fay tried
playwriting in 1939 and collaborated with Sinclair Lewis on
the play ANGELA IS 21, which was later filmed by Universal
as THIS IS THE LIFE, but the effort was only marginally
successful. Fay had starred in the Broadway plays NIKKI
and THE BROWN DANUBE in 1931 and appeared in the plays
GOLDEN WINGS and MR. BIG in 1941, but neither endeavor
was a success. After a few more "B" pictures, she married
screenwriter Robert Riskin (the union eventually produced
two children, Victoria and Robert, Jr.) and retired.

Her second marriage was a happy one, but Robert
Riskin died tragically in 1955 as the result of a brain em-
bolism. Fay returned to movies in supporting roles, often
quite effectively, and continued to work in films until 1958,
after which she appeared regularly in guest roles on television through the mid-sixties. Although she officially retired in 1965, she returned in support of Henry Fonda and
John Houseman in the TV movie GIDEON'S TRUMPET in 1980.
Fay is married to neurosurgeon Sanford Rothenberg, whom
she wed in 1971, and currently lives in Los Angeles. Fay
Wray's autobiography is in preparation as of this writing.

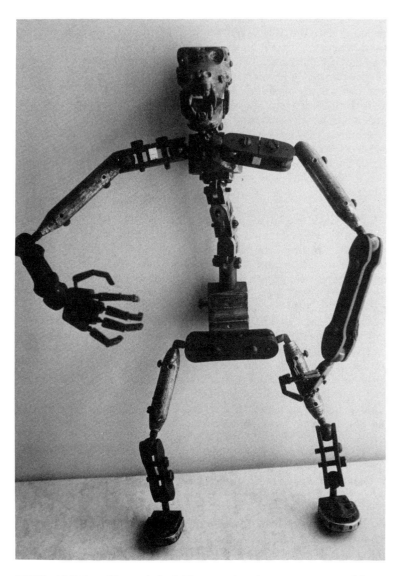

KING KONG: The original Kong animation armature, without covering, as it appears today. (Photo courtesy of Bob Burns.)

Robert Armstrong contributes a vastly entertaining performance as Carl Denham. His approach to the role is hardly
serious, and the film is all the better for it. Armstrong is
particularly effective in the scene aboard The Venture en
route to Skull Island, when he reveals a map of the ship's
destination. This seldom discussed scene is highly evoca-
tive, with the forboding little map, shown in close-up, and
Armstrong's description of the island and the mysterious wall
providing an ominous hint of the dangers awaiting them.
The acting of Armstrong, Frank Reicher, and Bruce Cabot
(whose inexperience is apparent in other scenes) is excellent
here, as the captain and his first mate initially scoff at Denham's revelations and are then slowly drawn into his compelling recital.

Honest and straightforward movies like KING KONG are
frequently misunderstood as being unsophisticated and are
criticized for not achieving "realism," which they are not
really trying to attain in the first place. But the alleged
sophisticates making these charges are usually either unin-
formed or, worse yet, intentionally dishonest in their criti-
cisms. The 1976 "remake" of KING KONG, which was not
really a remake at all, but a spoofy send-up, was so corrupt
and so diffused by its negative, low-brow "camp" approach
that it completely dissipated the mythic, larger-than-life potential of the original material and is already forgotten, despite having mysteriously won (amidst a storm of controversy)
an Oscar for its atrocious special effects. Surprisingly, star
Jessica Lange managed to survive her debut in this contempti-
ble debacle and went on to become an Academy Award winner
for her efforts in subsequent films.

Some footage from KING KONG was censored when the
picture was first reissued in 1938. The material included
shots of the brontosaurus mangling the sailors, the lengthy
scene in which Kong partially disrobes Fay Wray, scenes of
Kong rampaging through the native village killing the terrified savages, and New York scenes in which Kong mauls a
victim outside the theatre and snatches a terrified woman from
her bed, casually dropping her to the street below. All of
these cuts, except for a couple of the brontosaurus shots,
were restored for the early 1970s Janus Films reissue. Although the footage still does not appear in most TV prints,
all copies of the film available on videocassette are intact.

Beautifully constructed by Schoedsack, the first 30 minutes of the picture is all relatively serene build-up; one gets to know the characters and care about them with the film growing darker in tone as the ship approaches the island, its dangers only hinted at previously. The camera set-ups and lighting are simple in these portions, growing more fluid and detailed when the girl is kidnapped and offered to the monster as a sacrifice. After Kong makes his first appearance (about 40 minutes into the film), O'Brien's effects, only used peripherally up to this point, take over. The film barrels ahead with steamroller energy in its middle third as Kong battles an array of the island's monsters in defense of his prize. Max Steiner's incredible score, O'Brien's visuals, and Murray Spivack's convincing sound effects all meld together into a single driving force, the perfect combination of image and sound. After the ape's capture, the pacing relaxes somewhat as the monster is exhibited in New York, building to a fever pitch again as Kong escapes and terrorizes the city with the girl once again in his grasp, leading to the delirious conclusion atop the Empire State Building.

Everything about KING KONG--the writing, the direction, the acting, and special effects--is larger than life, aiming for a fairy tale, storybook quality that this technically complicated and overpoweringly effective picture achieves with deceptive ease. Like the best fairy tales that it successfully emulates, KING KONG is timeless, an enduring monument to the best that movies can offer.

KING KONG was Willis O'Brien's finest hour. After a number of failed projects that never materialized, O'Brien worked on one more major film, MIGHTY JOE YOUNG, in 1949. A gentle, whimsical fantasy loosely based on the Kong concept, MIGHTY JOE YOUNG presents the story of an inexplicably huge African gorilla raised and trained by an explorer's daughter. Produced by Cooper and directed by Schoedsack, the film starred Terry Moore, with Robert Armstrong as brash showman Max O'Hara in a virtual reprise of his Carl Denham role, and featured fine stop-motion animation by O'Brien and Ray Harryhausen, who actually animated about 85 percent of the picture. O'Brien received a well-deserved Oscar for the film. The rest of his career was spent toiling on low-budget science-fiction and horror films, many of which were ironically produced in response to the highly successful 1952 reissue of KING KONG. In his last years, O'Brien toyed with the idea of reviving King Kong in a film pitting the giant ape against an animated version of the Frankenstein monster. Attempting to secure permission for use of the Kong character from RKO, the project was taken out of his hands and licensed to the Japanese Toho Studios, which used O'Brien's concept as the basis for the juvenile film KING KONG VS. GODZILLA (see Chapter 17). Willis O'Brien passed away in 1962.

For further information on KING KONG, the reader is referred to THE MAKING OF KING KONG (A.S. Barnes & Co., 1975), by Orville Goldner and George Turner. This fascinating and enjoyable book is a credit to both its authors and a fine tribute to a wonderful film.

4. SON OF KONG

RKO, 1933

Credits:

Executive Producer: Merian C. Cooper
Director: Ernest B. Schoedsack
Screenplay: Ruth Rose
Camera: Eddie Linden, Vernon L. Walker, and J.O. Taylor
Special Effects: Willis O'Brien
Technical Staff: E.B. Gibson, Marcel Delgado, Carroll Shepphird, Fred Reefe, and W.G. White
Art Technicians: Mario Larrinaga and Byron L. Crabbe
Music: Max Steiner
Sound: Murray Spivack and Earl A. Wolcott
Set Design: Van Nest Polglase and Al Herman
Editor: Ted Cheesman
Associate Producer: Archie Marshek

Cast:

Robert Armstrong (Carl Denham)
Helen Mack (Hilda Peterson)
Frank Reicher (Captain Englehorn)
John Marston (Hellstrom)
Victor Wong (Charlie)
Ed Brady (Red)
Lee Kohlmar (Mickey)
Clarence Wilson (Peterson)
Katherine Ward (Mrs. Hudson)
Gertrude Short (reporter)
Gertrude Sutton (servant)
James B. Leong (Chinese trader)

Noble Johnson (native chief)
Steve Clemente (witch king)
Frank O'Connor (process server)
Constantine Romanoff (Bill)

Always casually pushed aside and somewhat overshadowed
by its predecessor, SON OF KONG is a very entertaining
film, and despite some opinions to the contrary, a worthy
sequel to KING KONG. Incredibly, RKO had this film on
theatre screens the same year as KING KONG with a December
1933 release, and part of the film's appeal is its immediate
connection to the original; the sets, music, and overall look
are in the same style, and Robert Armstrong's Carl Denham
character is expanded and acquires greater depth in this
follow-up adventure.

Oddly, Fay Wray and Bruce Cabot do not appear in
SON OF KONG. Following as quickly as it does on the heels
of the original, one would expect at least a brief cameo scene
of Cabot and Miss Wray, or perhaps a reference to them from
Denham. When asked about the matter for this book, Miss
Wray informed the author that there was never any discussion
of her appearing in the film. Possibly budgetary considera-
tions were a factor in this decision, since the sequel was con-
siderably less expensive than the original. Unlike Robert
Armstrong, Fay Wray was not under contract to the studio,
and casting a free-lance actress may have been considered a
strain on the budget.

SON OF KONG opts for a different type of story than
its parent film and begins on an amusing note as Carl Denham is ensnared in law suits and a grand jury indictment
resulting from Kong's rampage. Desperate, he joins forces
with Captain Englehorn, and the two set sail for the South
Pacific, intending to make a living hauling cargo with Englehorn's freighter. At an isolated port Denham meets Hellstrom, the Norwegian captain who had originally sold him the
map of Skull Island. Unknown to Denham, Hellstrom has
murdered the father of Hilda Peterson, an attractive per-
former in a local show, and seeking escape, concocts a story
about hidden treasure on Skull Island. Believing Hellstrom's
yarn, Denham and Englehorn set sail with Hellstrom for Skull
Island, not aware until they are at sea that Hilda is a stow-
away. There is a mutiny by the crew en route, and the four

SON OF KONG: Little Kong battles a monster, as Robert
Armstrong and Helen Mack watch from the altar.

of them, along with the ship's cook, Charlie, are set adrift
in a row boat.   Approaching the island, they are driven off
by the natives, who are understandably angered at Denham
after his previous visit, but they are able to land on the
other side of the island after rowing through a narrow chan-
nel.

        Separated from the rest of the party, Denham and Hilda
discover Kong's friendly offspring, who protects them from
the island's monsters and leads them to a temple treasure
which, despite Hellstrom's lie, actually does exist.   In the
picture's exciting conclusion, the treacherous Hellstrom is
devoured by a sea monster and the island crumbles apart in
an earthquake, with Kong's son sacrificing his own life by

SON OF KONG: Little Kong fights the cave bear.

holding Denham above the rising water until Hilda, Englehorn, and Charlie arrive in a row boat.   Adrift at sea, they
are eventually rescued by a ship.

Half an hour shorter than the original ape movie, SON
OF KONG is a small-scale adventure, striving for whimsy
rather than overpowering thrills.   Taken on its own dimunitive terms, this engaging film works rather well.   Although
Denham and party do not even reach Skull Island until the
last 20 minutes of the picture, the effects on display are
spectacular, and in a few instances the composite photography
is superior to many similar shots in the first movie.   A styracosaurus that fell to the cutting room floor in KING KONG
is on hand, as well as a huge cave bear, a fictional giant
saurian created by Marcel Delgado, and a sea serpent.   The
apocalyptic destruction of the island in the concluding earthquake is contrived, but fascinating, as the ground is rent
asunder and mountains crumble in an impressive display of

SON OF KONG: Willis O'Brien animating a monoclonius, which
does not appear in the film.

stop-motion animation, slow-motion miniatures, composite photography, and rear projection. Things are a bit rushed in this conclusion; the fate of Noble Johnson and his tribe is covered in one brief shot, as the shrieking natives tumble ignominiously into a crevice.

Although Willis O'Brien receives "chief technician" credit in the opening titles, much of the animation was actually handled by his KING KONG assistant, E. B. "Buzz" Gibson, who filled in when O'Brien was unable to work due to misfortune in his private life. (In a tragic act, O'Brien's wife shot and killed their two sons, and then turned the gun on herself.)

On initial release, SON OF KONG earned big grosses during its opening week, after which business sharply declined because audiences were disappointed in the picture, expecting a duplicate of KING KONG. Despite its relative obscurity, SON OF KONG is a pleasing addition to KING KONG, and unlike most sequels, at least attempts a different approach instead of merely repeating the highlights of the original. An entertaining picture, SON OF KONG certainly deserves better than the general neglect it has suffered.

5. ONE MILLION B.C.

United Artists, 1940

Credits:

Producer: Hal Roach
Directors: Hal Roach, Hal Roach, Jr., and D.W. Griffith
    (uncredited)
Screenplay: Mickell Novak, George Baker, and Joseph Frick-
    ert; based on a story by Eugene Roche
Camera: Norbert Brodine
Special Effects: Roy Seawright, Frank William Young, Fred
    Knoth, Danny Hall, Jack Shaw, and Elmer Raguse
Art Director: Charles D. Hall
Music: Werner R. Heymann
Makeup: Ben Madsen
Editor: Ray Snyder

Cast:

Victor Mature (Tumak)
Carole Landis (Luana)
Lon Chaney, Jr. (Akhoba)
John Hubbard (Ohtao)
Jacqueline Dalya (Ataf)
Nigel de Brulier (Peytow)
Mamo Clark (Nupondi)
Edgar Edwards (Shakana)
Mary Gail Fisher (Wandi)
Inez Palange (Tohana)
Jean Porter (girl)
Conrad Nagel (narrator)

ONE MILLION B.C.: Victor Mature and Carole Landis battle
a magnified lizard in this composite publicity photo. There
is no corresponding scene in the film.

Also known under the titles THE CAVE DWELLERS and
MAN AND HIS MATE, ONE MILLION B.C., surpassed only by
KING KONG, is one of the most artistically successful fantasy
adventure films of the sound era. Beginning with a prologue
in which leads Victor Mature and Carole Landis are shown as
modern counterparts of their prehistoric selves (thus cleverly
establishing audience identification with the two main charac-
tures), the film is a simple tale of two rival prehistoric tribes
which eventually unite to battle a common menace in the form
of a huge dinosaur threatening their existence. In its sim-
plicity the picture achieves a larger than life stature through
its poetic direction and fairy-tale special effects.

Exactly who directed the movie has long been a subject
of controversy. Renowned pioneering director D.W. Griffith,
then at the tragic end of his career, was employed by producer Hal Roach for the production. It has been established

that he cast the film, choosing Victor Mature and Carole Landis for the leads, and that he was involved in a nebulous,
supervisory capacity before filming began. The actual onscreen credits, however, read "directed by Hal Roach and
Hal Roach, Jr."; Griffith's name is absent; and to this day
veteran producer Roach denies that Griffith made any sub-
stantial contribution to the film. When asked about ONE
MILLION B.C. for this book, actress Jean Porter, who plays
the young girl cornered in a tree by the marauding tyrannosaurus, told this writer that Griffith did direct the film. As
Miss Porter recalls, "Yes--ONE MILLION B.C. was D.W. Griffith's last film. He was the director. I, too, have heard
others mentioned. Silly! I loved doing that film."

Certainly the picture's whole directorial style, the emo-
tional performances, the often poetic visuals and the sweep-
ing camera movements exhibiting an affinity for landscapes
and cloud formations, are Griffith's: the transitional pans
across the sky; the long, unbroken dolly shot following Victor Mature as he floats unconcious on a tree downriver, first
through a dark nightmare world of monsters, then into the
more brightly lit world of Carole Landis' tribe; and the lovely
introductory shot of Miss Landis, first glimpsed behind a cur-
tain of hanging leaves with only her legs visible. The film
has great power, a raw, boundless energy that is infectious.
This is red-blooded adventure at its best, laced with moments
of genuine beauty and tremendously effective on every level.

The art direction by Charles D. Hall (who contributed
to many of the classic 1930s Universal horror films) is impressive, as is the bright, crystal clear cinematography by
Norbert Brodine. The music score, by Werner R. Heymann,
adds immeasurably to the film, matching the lush visuals with
heroic flourishes, lyrical romantic themes, and low, rumbling
passages for the more threatening dramatic scenes involving
the monsters.

The special effects by Fred Knoth, with Roy Seawright
in charge of process photography, are engaging and remain
some of the finest examples of live-action slow-motion miniature work on film. The various reptiles used, convincingly
outfitted with rubber appliances representing horns and fins,
look truly menacing, and the rear-projection employed to en-
large them in relation to the actors is amazingly clear in most
scenes. Elephants dressed in fur coverings are used to

ONE MILLION B.C.: Caveman Lon Chaney and mate flee from
an enlarged lizard (no corresponding scene appears in the
film).

represent woolly mammoths, and the previously described
scene in which a young girl (Jean Porter) is threatened by
a tyrannosaurus while picking fruit in a tree uses a stuntman
(Paul Stader) in a rubber dinosaur costume to represent the
monster. Although the suit was only a rough prototype,
originally intended to be replaced by a more detailed version
for actual filming, it is well designed and looks firm, but the
figure is too restricted in movement and seems dimunitive and
rather pathetic in relation to the human cast. When Victor
Mature attacks and kills the tyrannosaurus with a spear,
quick editing and obscuring tree branches are used to conceal the outfit's deficiencies, with only partial success.

     Victor Mature, seldom an impressive actor, seems to
have been cast as Tumak on the basis of his rugged face
and impressive physique, although he is acceptable in the

ONE MILLION B.C.:   Prehistoric lovers Victor Mature and
Carole Landis.

role and even manages a degree of humor in a couple of
scenes.   Lovely Carole Landis was cast as Luana by Griffith
when he tested a number of women by directing them to run
a brief distance across the Roach lot.   Miss Landis looked
the most athletic and natural during her brief sprint and won
the role.   Lon Chaney, Jr. registers strongly as Akhoba,
Tumak's father.   Heavily disguised by makeup (Chaney is
successfully doubled by stuntman Yakima Canutt when he
hunts and wrestles a musk-ox single-handedly in an exciting
scene), Chaney is an imposing figure.   Shortly after ONE
MILLION B.C. he would enjoy success as the star of a number
of Universal Pictures horror movies, such as THE WOLF MAN
(1941).

A huge success on initial release, ONE MILLION B.C.
had a bizarre afterlife.   Hal Roach made the film's effective
monster scenes available to countless low-budget horror and

ONE MILLION YEARS B.C.: Raquel Welch cringes before a
hungry allosaurus.

science-fiction productions over the years, and the footage
was seen in films as diverse as TARZAN'S DESERT MYSTERY
(1943) and the Three Stooges short SPACESHIP SAPPY (1957).
Ed Bernds, who directed many of the Bowery Boys and Blon-
die second features as well as Three Stooges shorts and a
few 1950s science fiction features such as RETURN OF THE
FLY (1959), remembers directing one such cheapie for Columbia called VALLEY OF THE DRAGONS (1961), based on the
Jules Verne novel CAREER OF A COMET. Using ONE MIL-
LION B.C. monster footage, Bernds was able to film the
picture for a mere $135,000 and, as he told this writer, "Even
Sam Katzman wasn't making them that cheap!" The most un-
orthodox use of the footage was undoubtedly its inclusion in
the grade-Z feature VAMPIRE MEN OF THE LOST PLANET
(1970). Because this film was in color, when the ONE MIL-
LION B.C. scenes were used to represent the monstrous
denizens of another world, the original black and white footage

ONE MILLION YEARS B.C.: Cave dwellers repel a brontosaurus.

had to be tinted red, this lurid hue unconvincingly explained
as an atmospheric condition of the planet!

        The 1966 color remake, ONE MILLION YEARS B.C. (so
titled to differentiate the new version from the original), was
a huge success when the canny publicity department at 20th
Century-Fox promoted rising starlet Raquel Welch's physique
in the ads. Shot from virtually the same screenplay as the
original, this version featured some fine animated dinosaurs
by Ray Harryhausen (and, oddly enough, one enlarged lizard), but somehow failed to match the power of the Roach
film. However, Harryhausen did improve on the tyrannosaurus sequence with a wonderful vignette in which an allosaurus invades the tribe's domain only to be impaled on a
sharpened pole by hero John Richardson. The monster is
carried forward by its own momentum and gored on the pole
held by Richardson in an amazingly realistic shot that elicited
spontaneous applause in many theatres. Perhaps the ideal
ONE MILLION B.C. would have been a composite of the two
versions; the animated dinosaurs of the Harryhausen remake
combined with the poetry of the 1940 original.

ONE MILLION YEARS B.C.:   A promotional ad.

6. THE FLYING SERPENT

PRC, 1946

Credits:

Producer: Sigmund Neufeld
Director: Sherman Scott (Sam Newfield)
Screenplay: John T. Neville
Camera: Jack Greenhalgh
Art Director: Edward C. Jewell
Music: Leo Erdody
Editor: Holbrook N. Todd
Makeup: Bud Westmore

Cast:

George Zucco (Prof. Andre Forbes)
Ralph Lewis (Richard Thorps)
Hope Kramer (Mary Forbes)
Wheaton Chambers (Lewis Havener)
Henry Hall (Billy Hays)
Milton Kibbee (Hastings)
James Metcalf (Dr. Lambert)
Eddie Acuff (Jerry Jones)
Terry Frost (Bennett)

PRC (Producers Releasing Corporation) was, in the hierarchy of Hollywood studios, at the very bottom of the totem pole. Cheaper than Monogram, PRC spewed out dozens of the most threadbare horror movies and westerns in the business, although the horror films often featured such eminently watchable actors as Bela Lugosi and George Zucco, who

found the star billing offered by little PRC more enticing than
the supporting roles then available to them at the major studios.

Zucco's THE FLYING SERPENT is a very enjoyable minor
horror effort; it is cheap and preposterous to say the least,
but entertaining nevertheless, largely due to Zucco's eye-
gleaming zeal in the villainous lead role. With characteristic
PRC economy, the picture is a virtual remake of THE DEVIL
BAT (1941), a PRC effort in which a mad scientist (Bela Lugosi) eliminates his victims with trained giant bats, which
strike when attracted by the scent of "shaving lotion" offered
to the hapless prey by Lugosi. In THE FLYING SERPENT,
Zucco uses the Mexican god Quetzalcoatl, a fictional prehistoric flying reptile, to achieve the same goals. His targeted
victims are baited with a feather plucker from the serpent,
who is angered that its plumage has been defiled; the monster
then attacks and kills whoever possesses the feather. Oddly,
neither Zucco nor anyone else in the film is amazed by the
existence of a reptile with feathers. In the outrageous conclusion, Zucco, his misdeeds discovered, flees into the Mexican hills pursued by his own creature, gingerly clutching one
of the deadly feathers despite being fully aware that it will
lead the monster to him!

Lugosi's devil bats were at least marginally plausible in
appearance, but the title monstrosity in THE FLYING SER-
PENT is so badly designed that it resembles nothing more
than a rigid stuffed toy, sliding across the screen on a wire
in pursuit of its victims. The Mexican god Quetzalcoatl, in
more convincing stop-motion animated form, turns up again
in Q (1982), directed by Larry Cohen. Although it has been
claimed that the Cohen picture (see Chapter 36) is a loose
remake of THE FLYING SERPENT, the use of the same Mexican deity is the only similarity between the two films.

Low-budget fodder that it is, THE FLYING SERPENT
is enjoyable 1940s exploitation fare. If the film's plot is stale
and the technical effects inadequate, the picture's honesty,
at least, is commendable.

[Opposite:] THE FLYING SERPENT. The unconvincing title
monster strikes.

7. UNKNOWN ISLAND

Film Classics, 1948

Credits:

Producer: Albert Jay Cohen
Director: Jack Bernhard
Screenplay: Robert T. Shannon and Jack Harvey; story by
    Robert T. Shannon
Camera: Fred Jackman, Jr.
Special Effects: Howard A. Anderson and Ellis Burman
Art Director: Jerome Pycha, Jr.
Set Decorator: Robert Priestly
Music: Ralph Stanley
Editor: Harry Gerstad

Cast:

Virginia Grey (Carol Lane)
Philip Reed (John Fairbanks)
Richard Denning (Ted Osbourne)
Barton MacLane (Captain Tanowski)
with Richard Wessel, Dan White, and Philip Mazir

     Shot in Cinecolor, UNKNOWN ISLAND is one of the more
interesting variations on the familiar "lost world" theme, and
certainly one of the most entertaining. The plot concerns an
expedition to an uncharted South Pacific island for the pur-
pose of photographing prehistoric animals rumored to be still
living there. When the husband and wife heading the expedition book a tramp steamer for the journey, the ship's loutish
captain becomes interested in her and complications ensue.

UNKNOWN ISLAND: Virginia Grey takes aim at an unconvincing ceratosaurus. Only three of these dinosaur costumes
were used to represent an entire herd through the use of
split-screen photography.

Their only guide is an alcoholic sailor who had been on the
island before and witnessed the death of his shipmates, killed
by the monsters there. The couple barely survives the expedition, and before the fadeout the captain and most of his
crew have fallen victim to the island's monsters, and the wife
has left her husband for their sailor guide.

     The monsters in the film are realized either through the
use of stiff mechanical mock-ups (a dimetrodon and brontosaurus) or by men in costumes (a herd of ceratosaurs). The
most bizarre creature on display is portrayed by Ray "Crash"
Corrigan, a popular "B" western cowboy star who also moon-
lighted by playing gorillas in everything from Three Stooges

comedy shorts to Flash Gordon serial chapters. Corrigan
plays a bloodthirsty giant sloth (apparently meant to be a
megatherium), his standard gorilla costume seen in dozens of
other movies slightly modified with the application of claws
and longer hair.

These monsters, created by effects technician Ellis Burman, are among the most inexpressive and unconvincing on
record, but what really embellishes the film and compensates
for the lack of technical finesse, at least somewhat, is the
Cinecolor photography. Cinecolor was an economical color
system similar in tonal range to the two-strip Technicolor
used in such early thirties pictures as DOCTOR X and MYS-
TERY OF THE WAX MUSEUM. The process was not as re-
fined as the Technicolor system, with Cinecolor release prints
carrying an emulsion on both sides of the film stock; thus,
part of the color was always slightly out of focus. Due to
its cheapness (being only slightly more expensive than black-
and-white filming), Cinecolor was often used to dress up
otherwise routine westerns and action films. In 1948, when
movies of a fantasy nature in color were comparatively rare,
UNKNOWN ISLAND was more impressive simply because of its
color than it is now (although color 16mm prints do survive
in private collections, the film is currently distributed to
television in black and white).

If the color does not entirely counterbalance the short-
comings of UNKNOWN ISLAND, the actors certainly do. Actors who are attractive and/or competent are usually a rarity
in this type of film, especially in the 1950s entries, however,
in UNKNOWN ISLAND Barton MacLane, an enjoyable heavy
in many Warner Bros. films of the 1930s and 1940s, does not
disappoint and delivers an enjoyably boisterous, loud-mouthed
performance as the lecherous Captain Tanowski. Virginia
Grey is nicely cynical, and Richard Denning is noteworthy
as the drunken sailor, both of them offering characters of
some depth in the sort of picture too often dominated by
banal stereotypes. In fact, if the film's special effects had
been as good as these actors, UNKNOWN ISLAND might have
been a minor classic.

8. THE JUNGLE

Lippert, 1952

Credits:

Producer: William Berke
Director: William Berke
Screenplay: Carroll Young
Camera: Clyde De Vinna
Art Directors: A.J. Dominic and P.B. Krisman
Music: Dakshinamoorthy and G. Ramanathan
Sound: S. Padmanabhan
Editor: L. Balu
Associate Producer: Ellis Dungan
Executive Producer: T.R. Sundaram

Cast:

Rod Cameron (Steve Bentley)
Cesar Romero (Rama Singh)
Marie Windsor (Princess Mari)
Sulochana (the Aunt)
M.N. Namblar (Mahaji)
David Abraham (Prime Minister)
Ramakrishna (young boy)
Chitra Devi (dancer)

A turgid adventure opus filmed in India, THE JUNGLE would be entirely forgettable if not for its plot involving rogue prehistoric mammoths on the loose. Prehistoric animals other than dinosaurs are infrequently used in movies, probably because the giant reptiles are more bizarre and generally

more visually impressive than the huge mammals of later prehistory. THE JUNGLE is one exception, although the mammoths on display are only elephants outfitted with fur coverings, a la the mammoth in ONE MILLION B.C.

Otherwise, THE JUNGLE is meandering and generally
uneventful, with far too much footage devoted to the sluggish
overland trek in search of the monsters. Protracted and un-
remittingly tepid, THE JUNGLE slips easily from memory.

9. THE LOST CONTINENT

Lippert, 1952

Credits:

Producer: Sigmund Neufeld
Director: Samuel Newfield
Screenplay: Richard H. Landau; story by Carroll Young
Camera: Jack Greenhalgh
Production Design: F. Paul Sylos
Music: Paul Dunlap
Sound: Fred Lau
Sepcial Effects: Augie Lohman
Editor: Phil Cahn
Associate Producer: Jack Leewood

Cast:

Cesar Romero (Major Joe Nolan)
John Hoyt (Michael Rostov)
Hugh Beaumont (Robert Phillips)
Chick Chandler (Lt. Danny Wilson)
Sid Melton (Sgt. Willie Tatlow)
Whit Bissell (Stanley Briggs)
Acquanetta (native woman)
Hillary Brooke (Maria Stevens)
Murray Alper (M.P.)
William Green (Simmons)

A top-secret government rocket has crashed atop a remote jungle plateau, and intrepid Major Joe Nolan (Cesar Romero) leads a band of soldiers and scientists in an attempt

THE LOST CONTINENT: The leads cringe as two animated
triceratops clash.

to retrieve the missile before the enemy discovers it first.
Amidst a welter of paranoid Cold War rhetoric, Nolan and his
men encounter living dinosaurs on the plateau.   The savage
animals kill several members of the expedition before their
mission is successfully completed and the plateau is destroyed
in an earthquake.

     Although generally dull and uneventful, THE LOST
CONTINENT at least deserves a nod of approval for attempting the use of stop-motion animation on a very low budget.
Although the monsters (a pair of triceratops, a brontosaurus,
and a pterodactyl) are crudely, hastily animated, with the
design of the models imparting unwanted cute, Disney-like
qualities to the figures, the stop-motion process at least allows the presentation of action that would otherwise be denied
a cheap film of this nature.   Exactly who animated these
dinosaurs is unknown; Augie Lohman is given credit for the
picture's general special effects, but it is uncertain whether
or not he was responsible for these monster sequences.

The original theatrical prints of THE LOST CONTINENT were tinted green during the plateau scenes. This not only embued these portions of the film with an eerie atmosphere, but also succeeded in concealing flaws in the animation. THE LOST CONTINENT is sloppily constructed, with Romero's expedition taking far too long to reach the plateau summit and get down to business. But there are still several very effective scenes, particularly one shot in which a member of the expedition accidentally plummets from the cliff and vanishes into the mist below, and an unnerving sequence in which standard comedy relief Sid Melton is devoured by a triceratops.

Although the movie's low budget is at times obvious, with the opening scenes of a military installation represented by stock footage lifted from ROCKETSHIP X-M (1950) and a conveniently deserted native village near the plateau inhabited only by shapely Acquanetta and a young boy, THE LOST CONTINENT at least strove to achieve some degree of quality, and if the picture fails to attain any real distinction, its aspirations, at least, are commendable.

10. UNTAMED WOMEN

United Artists, 1952

Credits:

Producer: Richard Kay
Director: W. Merle Connell
Screenplay: George W. Sayre
Camera: Glen Gano
Special Effects: Paul Sprunk and Alfred Schmid
Art Director: Paul Sprunk
Sets: James R. Connell
Music: Raoul Kraushaar
Editor: William Connell

Cast:

Mikel Conrad (Steve)
Doris Merrick (Sondra)
Richard Monahan (Benny)
Mark Lowell (Ed)
Morgan Jones (Andy)
Midge Ware (Myra)
Judy Brubaker (Valdra)
Carol Brewster (Tennus)
Autumn Rice (Cleo)
Lyle Talbot (Col. Loring)
Montgomery Pittman (Prof. Warren)
Miriam Kaylor (Nurse Edmunds)

    A cheap exploitation film, UNTAMED WOMEN offers yet another retread of the standard "lost world" theme. When

their plane is crippled, members of an Air Force crew are
stranded on an uncharted island inhabited by prehistoric
monsters and a tribe of primitive women. In itself, the movie
is unremarkable; it is sloppily filmed, contrived, and unintentionally amusing. What is noteworthy (besides the array
of female beauty on display, which was, of course, the picture's selling point) is the film's excellent use of stock footage from ONE MILLION B.C.

The monster footage from Roach's film was made available to many low-budget producers over the years, but in
UNTAMED WOMEN outtakes and extensions of scenes not
used in ONE MILLION B.C. are seen, and footage originally
used as rear-projection backgrounds in the Roach movie are
seen as unadorned shots here. The filmmakers also deserve
credit for their efforts to integrate the UNTAMED WOMEN
cast into some of this stock footage; split-screens are used
surprisingly well throughout to insert the new performers
into frame areas formerly occupied by Victor Mature and
Carole Landis.

This optical printing, which at least allows greater flexibility than is usually possible with the use of stock footage,
is the only glimmer of quality to be found in UNTAMED WOM-
EN. Due to the ONE MILLION B.C. outtakes, the film's only
true value is as a curio for film buffs and historians.

11. THE BEAST FROM 20,000 FATHOMS

Warner Bros., 1953

Credits:

Producer: Jack Dietz
Director: Eugene Lourie
Screenplay: Louis Morheim, Fred Freiberger, Eugene Lourie, and Robert Smith; based on a short story by Ray Bradbury
Camera: Jack Russell
Special Effects: Ray Harryhausen
Production Design: Eugene Lourie
Art Director: Horace Hough
Music: David Buttolph
Sound: Max Hutchinson and George R. Grover
Associate Producers: Hal E. Chester and Bernard W. Burton

Cast: Paul Christian (Prof. Tom Nesbitt)
Paula Raymond (Lee Hunter)
Cecil Kellaway (Dr. Thurgood Elson)
Kenneth Tobey (Col. Jack Evans)
Donald Woods (Capt. Phil Jackson)
Jack Pennick (Jacob)
Ross Elliott (George Ritchie)
King Donovan (Dr. Ingersoll)
Frank Ferguson (Dr. Morton)
Mary Hill (Miss Nelson)
Michael Fox (Doctor)
Lee Van Cleef (Cpl. Stone)
Steve Brodie (Sgt. Loomis)
with Ray Hyke, Alvin Greenman, and James Best

THE BEAST FROM 20,000 FATHOMS: The monster's first
appearance (frame enlargement).

After the relative commercial failure of MIGHTY JOE
YOUNG (the picture cost approximately $2 million, with the
moderate grosses hardly justifying such an expenditure), it
was clear to Ray Harryhausen that if stop-motion animation
were to continue as an economically viable process in film
production, necessary changes were in order. In terms of
the personnel and materials involved, stop-motion animation
was, and is today, a comparatively inexpensive technique,
but the process is unavoidably tedious and time consuming,
and in film production, time, more than any other commodity,
is money.

By the early 1950s, the old studio system of movie-
making, with performers and technicians constantly available
under exclusive contract to their respective studios, was just

beginning to crumble. The studios had been divested of
their lucrative theatre chains by a landmark Supreme Court
ruling, and stronger unions had escalated production costs.
It was obvious to Harryhausen that the intricate Willis O'Brien
methods of sandwiching animation models between opulent
glass paintings and incorporating miniature projection screens
into the scale-model sets would have to be replaced by more
streamlined techniques.

The special effects for THE BEAST FROM 20,000 FATH-
OMS were produced very inexpensively, but through the use
of economical process photography and a few simple mattes,
Harryhausen, working with leftover equipment from MIGHTY
JOE YOUNG, was able to integrate his animated monster into
actual scenery, creating spectacular and highly effective
scenes of terror and destruction without resorting to the expensive construction of highly detailed miniature sets.   Ray

THE BEAST FROM 20,000 FATHOMS: The animated monster
on a miniature dock with the background added by rear-
projection.

Harryhausen may not have advanced stop-motion in an artis-
tic sense, but from a technological point of view his progres-
sive thinking at this time simplified the process, and at least
sustained its feasibilty with producers. In this sense--the
introduction of simplified and less costly high-quality stop-
motion animation procedures--THE BEAST FROM 20,000 FATH-
OMS is something of a technical milestone.

The plot for THE BEAST FROM 20,000 FATHOMS was
suggested by a Ray Bradbury short story of the same title
(later retitled "The Foghorn") about a lone surviving dinosaur attracted to a lighthouse foghorn because it believes it
is hearing another of its species beckoning. This sensitive
vignette was a poetic, effective mood piece, but hardly contained enough material for feature film treatment. The movie
simply uses the Bradbury story's basic concept--a living
dinosaur--as a statring point, and, although the lighthouse
scene previously described is used, presents the material in
a much more prosaic and conventional manner. In the film,
a slumbering prehistoric rhedosaurus (an entirely fictional
species) is released from its glacial Arctic tomb by an atomic
test blast and journeys south where it ravages Manhattan in
King Kong fashion until it is finally cornered by army patrols
at Coney Island. There, the monster is dispatched by a
radioactive isotope mounted in a rifle shell and fired into its
throat by a sharpshooter. Thrashing about near roller-
coaster tracks in an extremely atmospheric scene, the roar-
ing animal finally dies shrieking in a resulting fire. An ingenious subplot reveals that the monster was infected with
a deadly virus fatal to man, thereby allowing the marauding
beast to claim a few hapless plague victims in economical
scenes not requiring its presence!

Directed by art director Eugene Lourie, an unusually
conscientious Poverty Row craftsman (Lourie also directed two
other similar films covered later in this volume, THE GIANT
BEHEMOTH and GORGO), the picture is somber and menacing
in tone, due in large part to Lourie's influence on the script.
He wrote a good deal of it and managed to inject atmosphere,
characterization, and believable dialog that would be regretfully overlooked by the producers of later imitations. The
actors, too, are slightly better than usual for this type of
low-budget film, with veteran scene-stealer Cecil Kellaway a
standout as a paleontologist who falls victim to the beast.
When Harryhausen's life-like animation takes over, though,

the picture really snaps to life. The daytime sequences of
the giant monster rampaging through real, brightly lit New
York streets are startling. Simply explained, this was accomplished by animating the monster as it was photographed
through a sheet of glass on which an opaque black matte (of
tape or paint) obscured areas occupied by buildings and
cars in previously shot live-action footage of terrorized
crowds. The animation completed, the unprocessed footage
was rewound to the beginning, and the crowd scenes were
refilmed through a reverse matte obscuring the opposite
areas of the frame, resulting in a perfect composite. This
and the other tricks involved are cleverly used; especially
memorable is a shocking view of the rhedosaurus devouring
a policeman. Throughout these scenes, Harryhausen's supple
animation breathes convincing life into the monster.

Produced independently for $210,000 in the wake of
RKO's successful 1952 reissue of KING KONG, THE BEAST
FROM 20,000 FATHOMS was bought (for $450,000) re-scored,
and released by Warner Bros., earning an impressive $5 mil-
lion for the studio. Although hardly original to begin with
(despite Lourie's convincing details), the film's basic plot
would seem even more dog-eared in later years through repetition in too many similar pictures. However, THE BEAST
FROM 20,000 FATHOMS demonstrated the effectiveness of
stop-motion animation in modestly budgeted film productions,
and from the 1950s onward through the late 1970s, Ray
Harryhausen would be the leader in his field.

12. THE CREATURE FROM THE BLACK LAGOON

Universal-International, 1954

Credits:

Producer: William Alland
Director: Jack Arnold
Assistant Director (underwater scenes): James C. Havens
Screenplay: Harry Essex and Arthur Ross; story by Maurice
    Zimm
Camera: William E. Snyder and Charles S. Welbourne
Makeup (monster design): Bud Westmore, Millicent Patrick,
    Jack Kevan, and Chris Mueller
Art Directors: Hillyard Brown and Bernard Herzbrun
Music: Hans J. Salter
Sound: Joe Lapis and Leslie I. Carey
Editor: Ted J. Kent

Cast:

Richard Carlson(David Reed)
Julia Adams (Kay Lawrence)
Richard Denning (Mark Williams)
Antonio Moreno (Carl Maia)
Nestor Paiva (Lucas)
Whit Bissell (Dr. Edwin Thompson)
Bernie Gozier (Zee)
Rodd Redwing (Louis)
Henry Escalante (Chico)
Julio Lopez (Thomas)
Sydney Mason (Dr. Matos)
with Ben Chapman and Ricou Browning (both as The Creature)

The ultimate 1950s movie monster, the amphibious prehistoric "gill-man" in THE CREATURE FROM THE BLACK
LAGOON is, despite being an entirely fictional creation, one
of the most convincing film menaces ever designed. This
monster costume cost several thousand dollars and was well
worth the money and effort; this is no man stuffed into a
rubber suit with zippers visible, but a totally believable
studio concoction. This form-fitting costume is one of the
few creations of its type that is scientifically plausible.
Whether the gill-man swims underwater or walks ashore (Ricou
Browning portrayed the creature in the underwater scenes,

CREATURE FROM THE BLACK LAGOON: A graceful Ricou
Browning in his natural element.

while Ben Chapman substituted on land) the monster is genuinely frightening.

The plot is simplistic: when the fossilized foot of an amphibious prehistoric creature is found in the Amazon jungle, an expedition seeks the remainder of the fossil and instead discovers a living specimen. Fascinated by the beautiful female member of the expedition, the monster kidnaps her and kills several of her companions before it is finally destroyed. Originally shot in crisp, polarized 3-D (the film was later reissued in the inferior, murky red/green 3-D process during the early 1970s), the picture is just as effective in the "flat" television version, thanks to the superior design of the monster and Jack Arnold's careful direction.

In recent years, Arnold, who also directed other superior 1950s science-fiction pictures, among them IT CAME FROM OUTER SPACE (1953) and THE INCREDIBLE SHRINKING MAN (1957), has been lionized by some film commentators, who have wildly overpraised the director, reading all manner of metaphysical and allegorical implications into his

CREATURE FROM THE BLACK LAGOON: The gill-man terrorizes Julia Adams.

work. But if Arnold is not exactly the cinematic genius his
supporters believe him to be, he is nevertheless a good, unpretentious craftsman, and certainly a better director than
many of his 1950s contemporaries.   In THE CREATURE FROM
THE BLACK LAGOON, Arnold successfully exploits basic
human fears in several scenes: fear of the unknown, fear
of what might lie waiting just beneath the placid surface of
a tropical lagoon.   The much discussed underwater "ballet"
sequence, in which shapely Julia Adams, wearing a white
bathing suit, cavorts in the water as the unseen gill-man
swims with her, matching her undulating swimming movements,
is lyrical and stunningly photographed.   Arnold's handling
of the actors is good at all times; most of the performances
are restrained and believable.

     THE CREATURE FROM THE BLACK LAGOON was so
successful that it spawned two sequels: REVENGE OF THE
CREATURE (1955), also directed by Arnold, and THE CREA-
TURE WALKS AMONG US (1956), directed by John Sherwood.
THE REVENGE OF THE CREATURE, one of the last movies
shot in 3-D, is a disappointing film, lazily rehashing the most
interesting scenes of the original as the gill-man is discovered
alive, captured, and brought to America for display in a
marina.   THE CREATURE WALKS AMONG US is not much better, although the film does offer a truly bizarre plot: the
gill-man is recaptured and injured by fire in the attempt;
after scientists operate on the monster and remove its scaly
epidermis, they discover that it is vaguely humanoid in form,
complete with an operative pair of lungs.   Held captive, the
surgically altered gill-man has now been transformed into an
air-breathing creature and plods about clad in what appear
to be pajamas for the remainder of the film.   Eventually it
escapes, and after a mild rampage, commits apparent suicide
as it stumbles back into the sea.

     Universal-International's severe alteration of the gill-
man's appearance in THE CREATURE WALKS AMONG US indicates that the studio saw no box-office future in the property.   Regardless, the monster's fate in this picture is one
of the strangest resolutions ever imposed on a film series
character, human or otherwise.

13. IT CAME FROM BENEATH THE SEA

Columbia, 1955

Credits:

Executive Producer: Sam Katzman
Producer: Charles H. Schneer
Director: Robert Gordon
Screenplay: George Worthing Yates and Hal Smith; story by
    George Worthing Yates
Camera: Harry Freulich
Special Effects: Ray Harryhausen
Art Director: Paul Palmentola
Music: Mischa Bakaleinikoff
Sound: Josh Westmoreland
Assistant Director: Leonard Katzman

Cast:

Kenneth Tobey (Pete Matthews)
Faith Domergue (Lesley Joyce)
Donald Curtis (John Carter)
Ian Keith (Admiral Burns)
Dean Maddox, Jr. (Admiral Norman)
Lt. C. Griffiths, U.S.N. (Griff)
Harry Lauter (Bill Nash)
Capt. R. Peterson, U.S.N. (Capt. Stacy)
Del Courtney (Asst. Secretary Chase)
Tol Avery (Navy intern)

    When Sam Katzman produced the Columbia serial SUPER-
MAN in 1948, he was content to represent the famed comic

IT CAME FROM BENEATH THE SEA: The impossibly huge
animated octopus attacks a dock area.

book character's amazing exploits through the simple expedi-
ent of editing crudely animated cartoon footage into the live-
action proceedings.   Such brazen economizing was par for
the course with Katzman, who was responsible for some of
the cheapest serials and "B" pictures ever made.   Katzman
was known derisively as "Jungle Sam" within the industry, a
snide reference to his many low-budget jungle pictures, most
of which were shot with little more than a few potted trees
and a rear-projection screen.   But even a producer as cynical as Katzman knew that by 1955, with the growing competition of television, theatrical movie audiences demanded at
least some payoff for the price of admission even with the
lowliest exploitation fare.   It was at this time that Katzman
produced two fantasy pictures featuring stop-motion animation
by Ray Harryhausen: IT CAME FROM BENEATH THE SEA
and EARTH VS. THE FLYING SAUCERS (1956).   Harryhausen's expert technical contributions to these two films may
be the only vestiges of quality ever to grace a production
bearing Sam Katzman's name, and notably, IT CAME FROM
BENEATH THE SEA initiated Harryhausen's lengthy and
profitable partnership with Charles Schneer, who produced
under Katzman.

IT CAME FROM BENEATH THE SEA is a simplistic monster movie dealing with a giant "prehistoric" octopus which
attacks San Francisco after its arousal from hibernation.
The only genuinely worthwhile aspect of the film, either before or behind the camera, is the animated monster, and as
usual, Harryhausen does not disappoint on a technical level.
Although the monster octopus is impossibly, almost comically,
huge (one immense tentacle would appear to dwarf Godzilla),
the scenes of the beast attacking the city, with its supple
appendages coiling through the streets in search of prey,
are fascinating and extremely well done, with Harryhausen
deftly blending the animated puppet into live-action city
scenes.   For reasons of economy, the animated octopus is
missing a couple of the traditional eight appendages, although
this is not readily apparent onscreen.   Amusingly, because
the San Francisco city government denied Harryhausen official permission to shoot his background scenes (apparently
fearing that these sequences of urban destruction would have
an adverse effect on the tourist trade), Harryhausen was
forced to surreptitiously film his live-action background plates
from the concealment of a truck.

Harryhausen's animation makes IT CAME FROM BENEATH
THE SEA something special, demonstrating in the process
that even the lowliest exploitation fare can sometimes rise
above expectations and avoid total disappointment.

14. KING DINOSAUR

Lippert, 1955

Credits:

Producers: Bert I. Gordon and Al Zimbalist
Director: Bert I. Gordon
Screenplay: Tom Gries; story by Bert I. Gordon and Al
  Zimbalist
Camera: Gordon Avil
Special Effects: Bert I. Gordon and the Howard A. Ander-
  son Company
Music: Mischa Terr
Sound: Rod Sutton
Editors: Jack Cornwall and John Bushelman

Cast:

Bill Bryant (Dr. Ralph Martin)
Wanda Curtis (Dr. Patricia Bennett
Douglas Henderson (Richard Gordon)
Patricia Gallagher (Nora Pierce)
Marvin Miller (narrator)

Hurriedly concocted by producer Bert I. Gordon for
only a few thousand dollars, KING DINOSAUR was inspired
by the 1952 reissue of KING KONG, hence the title. Gordon
would have done well to emulate some of KING KONG's quality
as well, for KING DINOSAUR may well be the worst film of
its type. The plot involves a team of scientists who investigate a rogue planet, Nova, which has entered our solar system. Traveling there in a spaceship, they are confronted by

KING DINOSAUR: A reptilian denizen of the planet Nova
pursues the cast.

the prehistoric beasts living on the planet, including a tyrannosaurus, the dreaded "King Dinosaur" of the title.

This movie's screenplay is aggressively ignorant. Not
only is Nova referred to as both a "planet" and a "star,"
but exactly what are prehistoric animals native to earth doing
on another world? This would imply parallel evolution, a
concept mind-boggling enough to interest any scientist, yet
the question is ignored by the film's protagonists.

The special effects are uniformly inept except for a
couple of brief stock shots from ONE MILLION B.C. News-
reel footage of a V-2 rocket is used to represent the spaceship, and the monsters are all enlarged reptiles and insects,
badly shot and sloppily combined with the actors. The tyrannosaurus is impersonated by an unfortunate iguana lizard,
propped up on its hind legs behind a concealing rock.

Perhaps Gordon deserves some credit for being able to create any kind of a film on this amount of money, but there is little cause for celebration over the results. Produced so cheaply that it could not help but make money, KING DINOSAUR succeeded only in turning a profit for its producer and in plunging immediately to the rock bottom of its genre.

15. THE ANIMAL WORLD

Warner Bros., 1956

Credits:

Producer: Irwin Allen
Director: Irwin Allen
Screenplay: Irwin Allen
Camera: Harold Wellman
Special Effects: Willis O'Brien and Ray Harryhausen
Art Director: Bill Tuttle
Music: Paul Sawtell
Narration: Theodore Von Eltz and John Storm

Irwin Allen's THE ANIMAL WORLD, an otherwise unremarkable documentary tracing the history of life on earth,
benefited enormously from a prehistoric sequence featuring
dinosaurs animated by Willis O'Brien and Ray Harryhausen.
These scenes were exploited heavily in the film's advertising
and are the sole reason the picture is remembered today. A
dynamic bettle between a ceratosaurus and stegosaurus is
the highlight, and these lively animals are impressively well
animated. Because of Allen's budgetary concerns, though,
some shortcuts were necessary. The dinosaurs were shot
using multiple cameras filming the set-ups from different
angles in order to provide maximum footage, and the models
were quickly animated at two frames per exposure instead of
one; some live-action puppets were also used for close-ups.
The monsters are a bit stiff anatomically since they were cast
around the armatures directly from molds instead of being
constructed by the more desirable but time-consuming build-
up method; also, there is no process photography or glass
art to lend depth to the miniature terrain. This is straight,

THE ANIMAL WORLD: A ceratosaurus attacks a stegosaurus.
The monsters here are live-action puppets used for close-ups.

virtually unadorned (albeit thoroughly well-done) table-top
animation, with the O'Brien-Harryhausen creations thrashing
their tails and leaping about the scale-model sets almost exactly as they did in O'Brien's THE LOST WORLD more than
thirty years earlier.

Due to its documentary nature, THE ANIMAL WORLD
is rarely seen today. The memorable dinosaur scenes were
used again, though, as a prehistoric flashback sequence in
TROG, a 1970 horror film starring Joan Crawford, which
concerned a surviving prehistoric ape-man discovered by
scientists.

THE ANIMAL WORLD: Ray Harryhausen with a ceratosaurus
model.

16. THE BEAST OF HOLLOW MOUNTAIN

United Artists, 1956

Credits:

Producers: Edward Nassour and William Nassour
Directors: Edward Nassour and Ismael Rodriguez
Screenplay: Robert Hill, Ismael Rodriguez, and Carlos Orel-
    lana; story by Willis O'Brien
Camera: Jorge Stahl, Jr. and Henry Sharp
Special Effects: Jack Rabin and Louis DeWitt
Art Direction: Jack DeWitt
Music: Raul Lavista
Editors: Holbrook Todd, Maury Wright, and Fernando Mar-
    tinez

Cast:

Guy Madison (Jimmy Ryan)
Patricia Medina (Sarita)
Eduardo Noriega (Erique Rios)
Carlos Rivas (Felipe Sanchez)
Mario Navarro (Panchito)
Pascual Garcia Pena (Pancho)
Julio Villareal (Pedro)
Lupe Carriles (Margarita)
Manuel Arvide (Martinez)
Jose Chavez (Manuel)
Margarito Luna (Jose)
Robert Contreras (Carlos)

THE BEAST OF HOLLOW MOUNTAIN: The animated allosaurus
in a miniature set.

In 1955, Willis O'Brien wrote an original story called
"The Beast of Hollow Mountain," and, after meeting with
producer Edward Nassour, sold the story for very little
money with assurances from Nassour that O'Brien would be
contacted to supervise the stop-motion animation when production began. When filming actually commenced, O'Brien found
that he had been eased out of the proceedings. Although he
was given credit for his original story, he did not do the
animation and could not even get past the front office to meet
with Nassour.

The 1950s were a hectic period for movie producers.
With the new competition from television, filmmakers understandably believed that they had to offer the public something
that television could not duplicate in order to entice them
into theatres. Even though simply writing better scripts
would probably have worked just as well, a confusing array
of wide-screen formats, color processes, and three-dimensional
techniques was offered to audiences by the suddenly gimmick-
crazed studios.

Edward Nassour was no exception. When THE BEAST
FROM HOLLOW MOUNTAIN was released, Nassour announced
to the media that the picture had been filmed in the "Regiscope" process, which, according to Nassour, fed actuating
impulses via computer to a mechanical figure (in this case
the film's dinosaur monster), thus bringing it to life for the
cameras. Inevitably, there was not one word of truth to
Nassour's extravagant claims, and "Regiscope," was, in fact,
nothing more than a brazen attempt by the producer to de-
ceive a gullible public.

Actually, the onscreen monster, a marauding allosaurus in a western setting, was animated by conventional stop-
motion methods, except for a few shots of the animal running,
which used the cumbersome technique of "replacement animation." Replacement animation involves the sculpture of several immobile figures, each posed in a slightly different posi-
tion. Each figure is photographed for one frame, then replaced by another, slightly different figure until the action
they have been designed to represent has been completed.
This method is often used for simplified cartoonish model
animation in children's films; when correctly used it provides
uncannily smooth movement. In THE BEAST FROM HOLLOW
MOUNTAIN the process works in those brief shots because

the movements of the allosaurus running are repetitive, and the cyclical action is easily adapted to the technique.

Aside from those few replacement animation shots, THE BEAST FROM HOLLOW MOUNTAIN offers nothing unique, technically or otherwise. The stop-motion is crudely done and is certainly not up to Willis O'Brien's standards. The film presents a basic storyline that was a recurring theme with O'Brien--cowboys versus prehistoric monsters--and although some elements of this concept are found in O'Brien's MIGHTY JOE YOUNG and the later Ray Harryhausen film THE VALLEY OF GWANGI (which was based on an unfilmed O'Brien story), it is unfortunate indeed that due to Nassour's shabby treatment of him O'Brien was not allowed to animate his own story for THE BEAST FROM HOLLOW MOUNTAIN.

17. GODZILLA, KING OF THE MONSTERS

Embassy, 1956

Credits:

Producer: Tomoyuki Tanaka
Directors: Inoshiro Honda and (U.S. Scenes) Terry Morse
Screenplay: Takeo Murata and Inoshiro Honda; story by
    Shigeru Kayama
Camera: Masao Tamai and (U.S. Scenes) Guy Roe
Special Effects: Eiji Tsuburaya, Akira Watanabe, Hiroshi
    Mukoyama, and Kuichiro Kishida
Art Director: Satoshi Chuko
Music: Akira Ifukube
Sound: Hisashi Shimonaga
Editor (U.S. Version): Terry Morse

Cast:

Raymond Burr (Steve Martin)
Takashi Shimura (Dr. Yamano)
Momoko Kochi (Emiko)
Akira Takarada (Ogata)
Akihiko Hirata (Dr. Serizawa)
Achio Sakai (Hagiwara)
Fuyuki Murakami (Dr. Tabata)
Ren Yanjamoto (Sieji)
Toyoaki Suzuki (Shinkiebi)
Tadashi Okabe (Dr. Tabata's assistant)
Toranosuki Ogawa (Company President)
Frank Iwanaga (security officer)
Haru Nakajima (Godzilla)

Although hard to defend in light of the many inferior
sequels and spin-offs that have followed it, the original Godzilla movie is certainly a worthwhile film. Released in Japan
in 1954 under the title GOJIRA, the movie was imported by
American producer Joseph E. Levine two years later. In-
vesting a paltry few thousand dollars for the Western Hemi-
sphere rights, Levine promptly grossed millions. This story
of a mythical dragon that rises from the sea to destroy Tokyo
was, like so many other 1950s giant monster movies, inspired
by KING KONG. Although GODZILLA, KING OF THE MON-
STERS repeated the main flaw of those other pictures, failing
to endow the central menace with any character or persona-
lity, thus losing badly needed audience sympathy for the
monster, the film is so good otherwise that this drawback
can, for once, be forgiven.

Director Inoshiro Honda imbues the picture with an
impressive atmosphere. When Godzilla first appears, obliter-
ating a native village on remote Odo island, he remains largely
unseen, and, arising from the sea at night during a violent
storm, the monster seems almost elemental. We are allowed
to see only brief glimpses of the huge beast, accompanied by
heavy, thunderous footsteps on the soundtrack and a frightening, cavernous roar echoing in the darkness. Because of
this initial reticence, when Godzilla finally is shown clearly
the revelation is all the more effective. In a clever shot,
the monster's dorsal plates are seen projecting over a hilltop,
and the impossibly huge beast (400 feet tall, we are informed
at one point) suddenly rears upright into full view, leering
at the islanders below.

Eschewing dimensional animation in favor of a costumed
actor (and a mechanical bust used in a few shots), effects
technician Eiji Tsuburaya manages some compelling visuals.
Honda wisely keeps his black-and-white photography darkly
lit and his camera at a low angle, overcranking to achieve
slow motion. The monster's actions are slow and ponderous;
this is a lumbering, unstoppable dreadnought, and the scenes
of mass destruction are powerful and effective. Only a couple
of scenes do not work, because of either inappropriate lighting (the scenes of Godzilla at sea, shot in a studio water
tank, are too brightly lit, for instance), or obvious, badly
scaled miniature work (an overturned helicopter during the
storm sequence). But overall, the effects are excellent, and
the process and matte work, though hardly perfect, are

GODZILLA, KING OF THE MONSTERS: Godzilla destroys
Tokyo.

remarkably ambitious. The mime of Haru Nakajima as Godzilla is subdued, exhibiting none of the increasingly comic acrobatic gyrations that the monster would be guilty of in the later, lesser films in the series. Contributing immeasurably to the picture's mood is the music composed by Akira Ifukube, which in different scenes underscores the action with militaristic themes, funereal dirges, and lyrical classical selections.

When Joseph E. Levine imported GOJIRA for American distribution, the picture was dubbed into English, re-edited (shortened by about 20 minutes from the original 98-minute running time), and in a desperate attempt to provide a recognizable American name for marquee value, new scenes were shot featuring Raymond Burr as an inquiring American reporter investigating the catastrophe. This new footage was directed by former (and subsequent) film editor Terry Morse --the remade credits for the film somewhat ungraciously listed the directors as "Terry Morse and I. Honda"--and was shot in one day. Although the addition of this footage was largely unnecessary, and Raymond Burr's marquee value in those pre-Perry Mason days was dubious at best, the actor does well enough with his rather thankless role. The scenes are unobtrusive until one sees the far superior Japanese version of the picture, which flows much more smoothly than the American version. Oddly enough, even though Levine shortened and recut the film, he did include one memorable scene that was omitted from the original Japanese prints--Godzilla's savage attack on a ferry boat.

Since Godzilla had been irrevocably disposed of (by a scientist's "oxygen destroyer," which disintegrated the monster's flesh) at the conclusion of the first movie, with his lifeless skeleton clearly visible onscreen, there was no plausible way he could be revived for a sequel; therefore a second, different Godzilla emerged from subterranean hibernation for the next picture and the following sequels. The first sequel, called GOJIRA NO GYAKUSHU (GODZILLA'S COUNTERATTACK) in Japan, was still relatively serious despite some intentionally comic interludes. When the film was released in America in 1959 it was retitled GIGANTIS, THE FIRE MONSTER by the distributor, Warner Bros., recut, and dubbed to provide more laughs. The title was reportedly changed in order to avoid paying royalties to the original producing company, Toho, for the rights to the name "Godzilla," and Godzilla was

referred to as Gigantis throughout the film. Warners changed
more than Godzilla's name, though, by adding an English
soundtrack that often sank into outrageous, intentional comedy.
At one point, a character exclaims "Oh, banana oil!" in frus-
tration, a remark which, if nothing else, reminds us that
when one appraises dubbed films, one must proceed with
caution, since the actors are speaking to us in words and
voices not their own.

KING KONG VS. GODZILLA: The series degenerates into
cartoonish mayhem.

        Godzilla's next appearance was in KING KONG VS.
GODZILLA (1963), called KINGU KONGU TAI GOJIRA in Japan.
Shot in wide-screen and grainy color, the picture had a title
that practically insured box-office success with children, but
little else of any serious value.   Godzilla is discovered alive
inside an iceberg (where he had been entombed at the conclusion of GIGANTIS, THE FIRE MONSTER) and eventually
clashes with the giant ape King Kong.   Whether the King Kong

depicted here is intended to be the King Kong is open to
question. Not only does Kong's demise at the base of the
Empire State Building in 1933 go unmentioned, but in order
to even the odds for his inevitable confrontation with Godzilla,
this Kong is much larger--nearly Godzilla's height--and is,
we are told, charged with electrical energy! this nonanimated
Kong, played by a wildly gesticulating fellow in a ratty vaude-
villian ape suit (with a telltale seam clearly visible around
the collar), lopes across the miniature countryside merrily
projecting cartoon lightning bolts at his reptilian adversary.
"King Kong is now electrified!" deadpans a straight-faced
commentator to the audience, and the picture irreversibly
degenerates into giggly insanity. The costumed gorilla actor
in this film, with his hideous, stiffly inexpressive face mask,
could hardly be considered a threat to the original KING
KONG, and was soon forgotten. (This sadly moth-eaten
Oriental Kong, redesigned somewhat, appeared in one other
Japanese film, KING KONG ESCAPES, in 1968.)

With his appearance in KING KONG VS. GODZILLA,
Godzilla was beginning to exhibit certain endearing qualities
that would eventually transform him into a sort of reptilian
hero. As the series progressed, becoming more and more
comedic, even Godzilla's features changed and softened until
the formerly terrifying monster became virtually a children's
pet: a huge, scaly, doe-eyed teddy bear who frequently
defended the earth from other monsters and even invaders
from outer space and, perhaps most importantly (at least in
financial terms), proved useful as a marketing tool for promoting a morass of toys licensed by the copyright owners.

By the mid-1970s, the series had finally sputtered out
into an endless stream of frantic monster battles and childish
scenes of petulant urban destruction. The Godzilla character
vanished until 1985, when a new film, GODZILLA 1985, was
released. A direct sequel to the original 1956 film (and ig-
noring the many interim sequels), the picture used footage
from the first movie in a flashback sequence and promised an
improved storyline and technical effects, but failed to better
the original (and, sadly enough, even some of the sequels)
on either level. In a bizarre repetition of history, Raymond
Burr reprised his role from the original; as in the first picture his scenes were inserted (and even more arbitrarily this
time) after the film was acquired for American distribution
by New World Pictures.

90

The increasingly juvenile Godzilla films have certainly entertained legions of children, but in the end result, the sequels only serve to prove the superiority of their source, the original GODZILLA, KING OF THE MONSTERS.

18. THE SHE-CREATURE

American-International, 1956

Credits:

Executive Producer: Samuel Z. Arkoff
Producer: Alex Gordon
Director: Edward L. Cahn
Screenplay: Lou Rusoff
Camera: Frederick E. West
Art Director: Don Ament
Music: Ronald Stein
Editor: Ronald Sinclair
Associate Producer: Israel M. Berman

Cast:

Chester Morris (Carlo Lombardi)
Marla English (Andrea)
Tom Conway (Timothy Chappel)
Cathy Downs (Dorothy)
Lance Fuller (Ted Erickson)
Ron Randell (Lt. James)
Frieda Inescourt (Mrs. Chappel)
Frank Jenks (police sergeant)
Paul Dubov (Johnny)
Bill Hudson (Bob)
Flo Bert (Marta)
Jeanne Evans (Mrs. Brown)
Kenneth MacDonald (Prof. Anderson)
Paul Blaisdell (She-Creature)

"Hypnotized!   Reincarnated as a monster from
Hell!   It can and did happen!   Based on authentic
facts you've been reading about!   The startling dis-
closures about reincarnation and age regression!"

So proclaimed advertisements for THE SHE-CREATURE.
A couple of years earlier, in 1954, Universal-International
had produced the now-classic CREATURE FROM THE BLACK
LAGOON in 3-D, and THE SHE-CREATURE was certainly one
of the better imitators to follow in the slimy wake of the gill-
man.   Although by no means as accomplished as its predecessor, THE SHE-CREATURE was nevertheless an enjoyable and
worthwhile film and remains so today.   The picture's flaws
are entirely forgivable considering the restrictions of time
and budget imposed on the production.   The fictional species
of prehistoric monster created for THE SHE-CREATURE, although certainly not as realistic as the gill-man, was, in its
own way, equally as memorable and proved a considerable
asset to this diverting tale of murder, hypnosis, and reincarnation, which was interesting enough to stand on its own
merits.

The story involves hypnotist Carlo Lombardi (Chester
Morris), who receives a great deal of publicity when he ac-
curately predicts several murders.   Lombardi's beautiful assistant, Andrea (Marla English), is under his psychic control, and when Lieutenant James (Ron Randell) and the police
investigate the murders they suspect Lombardi, although they
are unable to prove anything.

A millionaire, Timothy Chappel (Tom Conway) sees
potential money in the hypnotism fad and forms a partnership
with Lombardi, promoting the hypnotist through newspaper
and radio coverage.   Chappel's wife (Frieda Inescourt) in-
vites her society friends to a demonstration by Lombardi at
their home.   Their daughter, Dorothy (Cathy Downs), is in
love with Dr. Ted Erickson (Lance Fuller), a research scientist who believes Lombardi is a fraud.   Despite his attach-
ment to Dorothy, though, Erickson is fascinated by Lombardi's
assistant, Andrea, and they become romantically involved.
Lombardi, aware of this, is jealous, but he is unable to prevent Andrea from Pursuing Erickson.

As a result of Timothy Chappel's promotion, Lombardi
is now nationally famous, but when another murder is reported,

THE SHE-CREATURE: The impressive monster costume designed by Paul Blaisdell.

Chappel orders Lombardi out of his home.   Finally, it is
learned that Andrea's other self, the hideous "She-Creature"
(Paul Blaisdell), brought forth when Lombardi exerts his
psychic power over her and returns her to a monstrous prehistoric incarnation, does his bidding and is responsible for
the murders.

     Lombardi orders Andrea as the She-Creature to murder
Erickson, but the monster fails to obey.   At the conclusion,
the She-Creature runs amok, murdering Chappel and Lt.
James; the monster then turns on Lombardi, killing him.   Before he dies, though, Lombardi finally releases the innocent
Andrea from his power, and the She-Creature, her other self
from the dawn of time, lumbers away into the sea.

The impressive monster costume for THE SHE-CREATURE
was created by Paul Blaisdell, who supplied make-up, special
effects, and props for many low-budget 1950s horror and
science fiction movies. The She-Creature costume, standing
6 feet, 6 inches tall and made of foam rubber and latex, was
constructed by Blaisdell and his wife, Jackie. The cumbersome outfit weighed 92 pounds and was designed with built-
in leverage, so that heavy weights (such as the She-Creature's
victims) could be lifted with relative ease. The heavy rubber
hide was thick enough to withstand the close-range firing of
.22-calibre blank ammunition. The outfit was unique and the
design managed to circumvent the almost unavoidable pitfall
of imitating the gill-man from CREATURE FROM THE BLACK
LAGOON, which was so functional in appearance that other
aquatic monstrosities of the 1950s, such as THE MONSTER
OF PIEDRAS BLANCAS (1958), couldn't help but plagiarize
the design to some degree. With the She-Creature, only an
incongruous pair of vestigal bat-like wings on the shoulders
and the unintentionally ludicrous female breasts (which, along
with the reptilian tail, where added at director Edward L.
Cahn's suggestion) detract from the overall effectiveness.

Recently, Alex Gordon, producer of THE SHE-CREATURE,
recalled the making of the film for this writer.

> It all got started at a Christmas party at the
> house of Newton "Red" Jacobs, who was the head
> of Crown International Pictures, when a local
> exhibitor suggested the title THE SHE-CREATURE.
> He didn't have any idea for a story, but he thought
> it would make a good title. At that time the Bridey
> Murphy case, the allegedly true story of a woman
> who revealed her past lives under hypnosis, was
> very much in the news, and Sam Arkoff's brother-
> in-law, Lou Rusoff, came up with a script.
> I wanted to get Edward Arnold and Peter Lorre
> for the picture because they had been in CRIME
> AND PUNISHMENT (1935) together. I thought that
> Lorre would be very good as the hypnotist, and
> Arnold as the businessman. They would be a good
> team, and also they were prestigious names for
> American-International at that time. Lorre, when
> he read the script, threw a fit and refused to do
> it, even though we already had a deal for his serv-
> ices through the Jaffe agency. At that time Lorre's

career was at a low ebb, and they had committed
him to the project even before he had read the
script. He just refused to do it, and even fired
the Jaffe agency as his agent over this.

So I was trying to think of a replacement. Edward L. Cahn, who was the director, had been
friendly with Edward Arnold. He had made a picture at M-G-M in 1944 called MAIN STREET AFTER
DARK with Arnold, Audrey Totter, and Dan Duryea.
He was going to talk with Arnold about doing THE
SHE-CREATURE, and we did make a deal with Arnold
for $3,000 to do the picture, but two days before
filming was to begin Arnold died.

We were all set to go on a nine-day schedule,
which is a very tight schedule, and we could only
afford a certain amount of time for cast members,
so this was a big shock. I tried to get John Carradine, but Carradine just threw a fit. At that
time he was on a big Shakespearean kick and had
just worked for Cecil B. DeMille in THE TEN COM-
MANDMENTS (1956) and didn't want to do any more
low-budget horror movies. In fact he practically
wrecked Lucy's restaurant--went on a drunken binge
and smashed up everything. He was absolutely impossible at the time.

So in the meantime I got Chester Morris, who I
knew because I met him at the Sea Cliff Summer
Theatre in New Jersey when I first came over here
from England. Chester was doing mostly stage work
at the time--he did DARK TOWER, which was the
stage version of THE MAN WITH TWO FACES (1934),
the Edward G. Robinson/Warner Bros. picture. I
asked him if he would play the role that Edward
Arnold was going to play, and he agreed to fly out
from New York for the week it would take to do it.
But now with John Carradine out of it I was really
pressed, so I asked Chester if he would take the
lead, the hypnotist role, and he agreed, even though
the role was a bit different from the type he was
used to. Chester was a very successful amateur
magician, in fact, virtually a professional quality
magician, and he had done charity appearances, so
it was a treat for him to play that role.

Tom Conway was flying over from England, where
he was supposed to do a picture for my brother, to

play the police inspector, and when he arrived at
the airport I asked him if he would take over the
part that Edward Arnold was going to play. I got
Ron Randell on the phone. He had just finished a
job here and had a week before he had to leave for
Australia, so I asked him if he wanted to pick up
a fast $750 and play the police inspector. He didn't
even know what the script was.

It was a mishmash of casting and not entirely
satisfactory. We went down to Paradise Cove near
Malibu for the shooting, where I got a tremendous
sunburn on the beach. Everything went smoothly
then, but those had been very traumatic times before starting the production. Unfortunately, it
turned out to be a very slow-moving picture, but
we had to have a certain amount of footage, and on
that kind of budget, $104,000, you can't have a lot
of action. You have to use a lot of dialog to fill
the time. It's kind of a fun picture--I had a lot
of old-timers in there--El Brendel, Jack Muhall, and
Luana Walters, who was with Bela Lugosi in THE
CORPSE VANISHES (1942).

Although Alex Gordon's production of THE SHE-CREATURE
will never be mentioned in the same breath with classics like
CREATURE FROM THE BLACK LAGOON, the movie is still
a tribute to the craftsmen and technicians who were able to
surmount budgetary restrictions and produce a solid, competent piece of entertainment. Paul Blaisdell, in particular,
laboring without the luxury of elaborate molding techniques
and the complicated mechanical appendages so common in more
recent films of this type, created one of the most impressive
of the low-budget 1950s movie monsters and deserves high
praise for the results.

19. THE BLACK SCORPION

Warner Bros., 1957

Credits:

Producers: Frank Melford and Jack Dietz
Director: Edward Ludwig
Screenplay: David Duncan and Robert Blees; story by Paul
  Yawitz
Camera: Lionel Lindon
Special Effects: Willis O'Brien and Pete Paterson
Art Director: Edward Fitzgerald
Music: Paul Sawtell
Sound: Rafael L. Esparza
Editor: Richard Van Enger

Cast:

Richard Denning (Henry Scott)
Mara Corday (Teresa)
Carlos Rivas (Arthur Ramos)
Mario Navarro (Juanito)
Carlos Muzquiz (Dr. Velazco)
Pascual Pena (Jose de la Cruz)
Fanny Schiller (Florentina)
Pedro Galvin (Father Delgado)
Arturo Martinez (Major Cosio)

THE BLACK SCORPION begins with an erupting Mexican
volcano, from which the giant title insect and others of its
fictional species emerge from the slumber of antiquity to rav-
age the countryside. The simple plot is comprised of standard

97

THE BLACK SCORPION.   The grotesque live-action head
used for close-ups.

monster movie elements with no surprises save for the novelty
of locale. What does make the picture work to a degree are
Willis O'Brien's superbly animated insect monsters, enhanced
by dark, nicely atmospheric photography. In films of this
type the lighting is frequently keyed just as low as the budget in an attempt to conceal production flaws; in this case
the brooding camera work is a definite asset.

The special effects are cheap, but nicely done. The
scorpions (which were animated by Pete Peterson, O'Brien's
assistant from MIGHTY JOE YOUNG, under O'Brien's supervision) are deadly, truly menacing creatures, scuttling over
the Mexican terrain with cunning malevolence. In one scene,
involving a descent into the volcano in order to combat the
scorpions, a giant spider, a leftover model from the cut spider

pit sequence in KING KONG, is used to good effect. The
actors, led by stalwart Richard Denning and lovely Mara
Corday, are good, but Edward Ludwig's direction of their
scenes is uninspired and made to seem even more so by
O'Brien's dynamic animation sequences.

The low budget did take its toll on some of the effects.
In one scene a lone giant scorpion survives to wreak havoc
on a town after the other monsters have been destroyed. In
these shots the traveling matte of the scorpion was printed
over the scenes of a fleeing crowd, without printing the fill-
in image, resulting in what appears to be a featureless black
shadow of the insect menacing the populace. For close-ups
of the scorpion's face, a live-action mock-up was constructed
and intercut with the animation shots. This hideous visage,
with its mouth constantly oozing drool, doesn't bear the
slightest resemblance to the animated model and is so grotesque in appearance and restricted in movement that its use
is detrimental to the action.

In spite of these flaws, O'Brien's craftsmanship is in
abundant evidence otherwise, particularly in the sequence
depicting a group of scorpions derailing a train and then
preying on the passengers. Bob Burns, an effects technician who once assisted Paul Blaisdell (creator of THE SHE
CREATURE) knew O'Brien at this time and visited him in his
workshop when this scene was being shot. Burns recalls
O'Brien as a warm and friendly man and remembers that for
this train wreck scene O'Brien had even installed tiny sil-
houettes of the passengers behind the lighted train windows,
so that these could be set in motion and provide the illusion
of frantic passengers inside the cars.

Such conscientious and detailed technical work is its
own justification and makes films like THE BLACK SCORPION
a little better than the run-of-the-mill exploitation fare they
would inevitably be without this sort of dedicated craftsmanship.

20. THE DEADLY MANTIS

Universal-International, 1957

Credits:

Producer: William Alland
Director: Nathan Juran
Screenplay: William Berkely; story by William Alland
Camera: Ellis Carter, Clifford Stine and Tom McCrory
Special Effects: Fred Knoth
Art Director: Robert Clatworthy
Music: William Lava; Music Supervision by Joseph Gershenson and Harris Ashburn
Sound: Vernon Kramer, Leon M. Leon, and Leslie I. Carey
Editor: Chester Schaefer

Cast:

Craig Stevens (Col. Joe Parkman)
William Hopper (Dr. Ned Jackson)
Alix Talton (Marge Blaine)
Donald Randolph (Gen. Mark Ford)
Pat Conway (Sgt. Pete Allen)
Florenz Ames (Prof. Anton Gunther)
Paul Smith (Corporal)
Phil Harvey (Lou)
Floyd Simmons (Army Sergeant)
Paul Campbell (Lt. Fred Pizar)
Harry Tyler (Spectator)

Arriving near the end of the 1950s boom of science fiction movies, THE DEADLY MANTIS is one of the weakest of the giant monster pictures and certainly the worst to emerge from Universal-International, which had offered THE CREATURE FROM THE BLACK LAGOON in better days. Slapped together from standard genre elements, the trite plot deals with an immense (ostensibly prehistoric) preying mantis which attacks civilization after an avalanche frees the monster from an iceberg.

Depressingly, the film offers nothing. Although quite bad, it is not bad enough to offer the negative entertainment of derision, and the hapless viewer is left adrift without even that dubious compensation. The leads (Craig Stevens, William Hopper, and Alix Talton) are so colorless that they are virtually invisible, and the technical work, although competent, is generally unremarkable. In most scenes the mantis is represented by a live-action puppet, although in some shots a real insect is used; inevitably, the live specimen proves more convincing than the studio concoction, which suffers by comparison.

Included here only as a comparative example, THE DEADLY MANTIS remains a bland vacuum and a painful reminder of just how mind-numbingly awful this sort of corporate paint-by-the-numbers film-making can be.

21. THE GIANT CLAW

Columbia, 1957

Credits:

Producer: Sam Katzman
Director: Fred F. Sears
Screenplay: Samuel Newman and Paul Gangelin
Camera: Benjamin H. Kline
Special Effects: Ralph Hammeras and George Teague
Art Director: Paul Palmentola
Film Editors: Saul A. Goodkind and Tony DiMarco
Music: Mischa Bakaleinikoff
Sound: Josh Westmoreland
Assistant Director: Leonard Katzman

Cast:

Jeff Morrow (Mitchell MacAfee)
Mara Corday (Sally Caldwell)
Morris Ankrum (Lt. Gen. Edward Lewis)
Louis D. Merrill (Pierre Broussard)
Edgar Barrier (Dr. Noyman)
Robert Shayne (Gen. Ben Penner)
Ruell Shayne (Pete)
Clark Howat (Major Spelling)
Morgan Jones (Lieutenant)

Even "B"-movie producer Sam Katzman, often justifiably maligned for his many low-budget exploitation pictures, could occasionally create a watchable film, as he did with IT CAME FROM BENEATH THE SEA, which featured some excellent

stop-motion animation by Ray Harryhausen. Unfortunately,
Katzman just did not care about most of his movies; his phi-
losophy was to make them cheap and fast, minimizing expenditure and maximizing profits for a quick turnover. THE
GIANT CLAW may be the quintessential Katzman monster
movie. Cheaply produced to begin with, Katzman farmed the
special effects work out to Ralph Hammeras and George Teague, who shot the footage in Mexico at the same time Willis
O'Brien was at work on the animation for THE BLACK SCOR-
PION at the same studio.

These effects for THE GIANT CLAW are horrendously,
laughably bad. The titular menace, a giant extraterrestrial
(and also, we are informed, prehistoric) bird that invades
earth, is so side-splittingly hilarious in appearance, with its
monstrously comical bug-eyed face and rigid feathered body,
that it looks like some deformed child's toy as it glides about
on wires wreaking low-budget destruction.

The actors, although quite adequate, are also compromised by the special effects. As square-jawed Morris Ankrum
looks stern and official as the general and hero Jeff Morrow
mouths pseudoscientific gobbledy-gook as he attempts to de-
feat the monster, they are blissfully unaware that their performances will collapse into unintentional parody when intercut with the outrageously inept special effects. Only Mara
Corday, who is on hand merely to look attractive, escapes
relatively unscathed.

As laughable as THE GIANT CLAW is, it should be remembered that Ralph Hammeras was one of Hollywood's finest
technicians. He worked with Willis O'Brien on THE LOST
WORLD (1925), contributed opulent, meticulously-detailed illusions to the futuristic JUST IMAGINE (1930), and won an
Academy Award for his contributions to Walt Disney's 20,000
LEAGUES UNDER THE SEA (1954), among his noteworthy ac-
complishments. The monster in THE GIANT CLAW is so aggressively cartoonish in design (for obvious reasons, Columbia released no publicity stills of this feathered menace), it's
hard to believe that at least some of its appearance wasn't
intentional, a sly jab, perhaps, at the film's crass producer,
who certainly received the monster he deserved.

22. THE LAND UNKNOWN

Universal-International, 1957

Credits:

Producer: William Alland
Director: Virgil Vogel
Screenplay: Laszlo Gorog; story by Charles Palmer, adaptation by William N. Robson
Camera: Ellis W. Carter and Clifford Stine
Special Effects: Fred Knoth, Orien Ernest, Jack Kevan, and Roswell A. Hoffman
Art Directors: Richard Riedel and Alexander Golitzen
Music: Joseph Gershenson
Editor: Fred MacDowell
Make-up: Bud Westmore

Cast:

Jock Mahoney (Commander Harold Roberts)
Shawn Smith (Margaret Hathaway)
Henry Brandon (Dr. Charles Hunter)
William Reynolds (Lt. Jack Carmen)
Steve Miller (Phil Harvey)
Douglas R. Kennedy (Capt. Burnham)

THE LAND UNKNOWN, shot in Cinemascope, is a competent and thoroughly watchable extention of the familiar "lost world" theme. The story involves a navy expedition, accompanied by the requisite attractive woman reporter, that journeys to an abnormally warm region of the South Pole which had been explored by a previous, unsuccessful expedition.

THE LAND UNKNOWN: A rigid mechanical plesiosaur attacks
Shawn Smith, adrift in a lifeboat, as her companions attempt
a rescue by helicopter.

Disembarking from an aircraft carrier, the team's helicopter
is damaged by collision with a pterodactyl and is forced into
the cone of a volcano. Descending through the mist, they
land and find themselves in a prehistoric world inhabited by
dinosaurs, as well as a surviving member of the previous expedition, who, driven nearly insane by his years of isola-
tion, lives like a primitive cave dweller. After harrowing
encounters with a tyrannosaurus and plesiosaurus, among
other monsters, they are eventually able to repair their helicopter, and, unlike the first expedition, safely return.

        Arriving as late as it does in the plethora of 1950s
science fiction movies, THE LAND UNKNOWN is an unusually
ambitious effort. The wide-screen, Cinemascope format, always tricky to work with in terms of visual composition, offers some impressive panoramic views of the prehistoric landscape. Shot in black-and-white, the preponderance of gray
tones suggests that the production may have been designed
with color in mind. Although lacking in some detail, the sets
are eerie and well designed.

Oddly, special effects technician Fred Knoth used three
different techniques to bring the film's prehistoric monsters
to life: magnified lizards in miniature sets, mechanical mock-
ups, and men in costumes. The result is a strange visual
hodgepodge that doesn't quite work. Knoth worked on ONE
MILLION B.C., and not surprisingly the live reptiles work
best here. Far less successful are the mock-ups representing a pterodactyl and plesiosaur; they are, as usual with
such contrivances, stiff and lifeless, and the plesiosaur, with
a permanent sneer etched on its face, is unintentionally comical. Worst of all is a costumed actor representing a tyrannosaurus. Not only is it impossible for a human being to
even approximate the stance and physique of such a creature,
but the suit is very badly designed in the bargain and looks
even worse than the ceratosaurus costumes in UNKNOWN
ISLAND. The head of this costume was later used to represent Spot, the reptilian pet of the ghoulish TV situation
comedy family in The Munsters. The performers are blended
into the monster action through Clifford Stine's generally

THE LAND UNKNOWN: Men in dinosaur costumes rarely convince, as this scene clearly proves.

well-done matte photography, although in some scenes this work suffers from the same flaw that marred Stine's similar efforts in THE INCREDIBLE SHRINKING MAN (1957): the contrast on the superimposed footage of the actors is much too light in relation to the background scenes.

The actors are acceptable. Jock Mahoney and William Reynolds are traditionally stolid as the leading heroes, with Henry Brandon more impressive as the wild-eyed survivor of the previous expedition. Blonde Shawn Smith, a rather good actress, was formerly known as Shirley Patterson in the early 1940s and was attempting a comeback of sorts in the fifties under her new name. As Shirley Patterson she is best known to film buffs for her charming presence in BATMAN (1943), a wild and woolly Columbia serial based on the popular comic book character.

Director Virgil Vogel, who also directed another Universal thriller, THE MOLE PEOPLE (1956), is generally unimaginative here and fails to bring any real style or pacing to the film. THE LAND UNKNOWN has all the right ingredients otherwise, and if the film had been more tightly directed (by Jack Arnold, perhaps) and more consistent technically, it would have undoubtedly been one of the more impressive "lost world" films.

23. THE MONSTER THAT CHALLENGED THE WORLD

United Artists, 1957

Credits:

Producers: Jules V. Levy and Arthur Gardner
Director: Arnold Laven
Screenplay: Patricia Fielder; story by David Duncan
Camera: Maurice Vaccarino and Scotty Welbourne
Special Effects: Augie Lohman
Art Director: James Vance
Music: Heinz Roemheld
Editor: John Faure

Cast:

Tim Holt (John Twillinger)
Audrey Dalton (Gail MacKenzie)
Hans Conreid (Dr. Jess Rogers)
Harlan Warde (Lt. Bob Clemens)
Casey Adams (Tad Johns)
Mimi Gibson (Sandy MacKenzie)
Gordon Jones (Josh Peters)
Marjorie Stapp (Connie Blake)
Dennis McCarthy (George Blake)
Barbara Darrow (Jody Sims)
Bob Beneveds (Mort Beatty)
Michael Dugan (Clarke)
Mac Williams (Capt. Mastera)
Eileen Harley (Sally)
Jody McCrea (Seaman Fred Johnson)
William Swan (Sanders)
Charles Tannen (Wyatt)

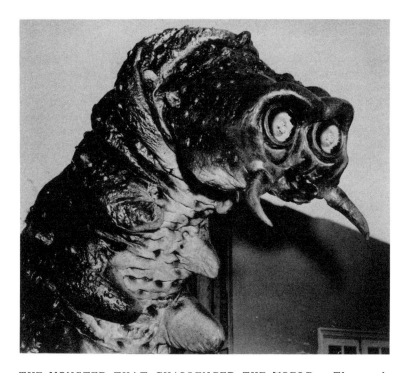

THE MONSTER THAT CHALLENGED THE WORLD: The mechanical sea monster.

Byron Kane (Coroner)
Hal Taggert (Mr. Davis)
Gil Frye (Scott)
Dan Gachman (Deputy Brewer)
Milton Parsons (Mr. Dobbs)
Ralph Moody (old gatekeeper)

The production team of Jules V. Levy, Arthur Gardner, and Arnold Laven concocted several interesting horror pictures in the late 1950s, including THE RETURN OF DRACULA (1958) and THE VAMPIRE (1958), in addition to THE MONSTER THAT CHALLENGED THE WORLD. Although these were low-budget films, Levy, Gardner, and Laven were a bit more conscientious than most of their peers, offering scripts and

direction that were a cut above the competition; THE MON-
STER THAT CHALLENGED THE WORLD is no exception.

The film, which deals with a giant prehistoric sea snail
that terrorizes a coastal area, has a standard monster-on-
the-loose plot, yet is enhanced by surprisingly good characterization, particularly from veteran actor Hans Conreid.
The titular monster, a life-sized mechanical mock-up constructed by Augie Lohman, is one of the few such movie contrivances that actually work; because of the monster's insec-
toid physique the limited body movements seem entirely appropriate.

The picture is intelligent and effective. The brooding
atmosphere in the night scenes helps a great deal, and the
monster's final attack on a mother and her young daughter
is well edited and exciting. In fact, the film holds up so
well that in the early 1970s, United Artists reissued THE
MONSTER THAT CHALLENGED THE WORLD on a double-bill
with THE RETURN OF DRACULA. Both films were printed
on color stock with a lurid green tint for this limited rerelease.

24. RODAN

DCA, 1957

Credits:

Director: Inoshiro Honda
Screenplay: Takeshi Kimura and Takeo Murata; story by
   Takeshi Kuronomura
English Dialogue: David Duncan
Camera: Isamu Ashida
Special Effects: Eiji Tsuburaya
Art Director: Tatsuo Kita
Sound: Masanobu Miyazaki
Music: Akira Ifukube
Editor (U.S. version): Robert S. Eisen

Cast:

Kenji Sawara (Shigeru)
Yumi Shirakawa (Kyo)
Akihiko Hirata (Dr. Kashiwagi)
Akio Kobori (Nishimura)
Yasuko Nakata (young woman)
Monosuke Yamada (Ohsaki)
Yoshimubi Tojima (Izeki)
with Kiyoharu Ohnaka

   The first of the Japanese monster films shot in color,
RODAN (titled RADON in Japan) is one of the better follow-
ups to GODZILLA, KING OF THE MONSTERS. Apparently
designed to resemble a pteranodon (the head in particular
is very similar), the winged monster appears in modern-day

RODAN: The title monster levels Tokyo.

Japan and promptly embarks upon the expected campaign of
mass destruction.   Impossibly huge, with a wingspan of several hundred feet, the airborne monster destroys everything
in its path, the sheer pressure of its beating wings resulting
in irresistible winds of hurricane velocity.   These apocalyptic scenes of urban destruction, with buildings exploding and
debris swirling in a violent maelstrom of carnage, are impressively filmed.   However, the garish, lurid color, although
initially appealing, works against the film in these portions;
everything is just too brightly lit.   As a result, the dark
nightmare atmosphere that enhanced GODZILLA, KING OF
THE MONSTERS is almost entirely absent here.

      The monster itself, represented by the usual actor in
a rubber costume, is impressive enough in most scenes, although in a few shots the outfit suffers from an unfortunate
"baggy pants" effect in the legs.   Some inanimate mock-ups
are used on occasion, but sadly, the long shots of the monster in flight are the most unconvincing, with Rodan leaving

an incongruous vapor trail in his wake. Otherwise, Eiji
Tsuburaya's scale-model slow-motion effects work is impressive, clearly defined and at times breathtakingly detailed.

Initially slated for release by RKO (the studio apparently did some post-production work on the sound track since,
interestingly, Fay Wray's KING KONG screams can be heard
at one point, as well as the shrieks of the sailors from the
spider-pit scene), the picture was eventually distributed by
DCA and was a considerable success. The floodgates were
opened, and Japan was soon buried under a veritable avalanche of grotesque rubbery monsters, among them Mothra
(the giant moth) and Gammera (the giant flying turtle). Although most of these increasingly tiresome behemoths were
either mythical or entirely fictional rather than prehistoric
in origin, the often preposterous explanations for their presence, intended to lend credence to their misadventures, did
little to convince an uninterested public. As with Godzilla,
the main value of these monsters has been to the prolific
manufacturers of children's toys.

25. THE GIANT BEHEMOTH

Allied Artists, 1959

Credits:

Producer: David Diamond
Director: Eugene Lourie
Screenplay: Eugene Lourie; story by Robert Abel and Allen Adler
Camera: Ken Hodges
Special Effects: Jack Rabin, Irving Block, Louis De Witt, Willis O'Brien and Pete Peterson
Art Director: Harry White
Music: Edwin Astley
Sound: Sid Wiles
Editor: Lee Doig
Makeup: Jimmy Evans

Cast:

Gene Evans (Steven Karnes)
Andre Morell (Prof. Bickford)
John Turner (Ian Duncan)
Leigh Madison (Jean MacDougall)
Jack MacGowran (Dr. Sampson)
Maurice Kaufmann (submarine commander)
Henry Vidon (Thomas MacDougall)
Leonard Sachs (scientist)

THE GIANT BEHEMOTH is noteworthy only because of Willis O'Brien's participation. In every other respect the film is a pale imitation of THE BEAST FROM 20,000 FATHOMS,

114

THE GIANT BEHEMOTH: An original promotional ad.

THE GIANT BEHEMOTH: The live-action model head emerges
from the river.

which was also directed by Eugene Lourie.   Unfortunately,
Lourie, with his invaluable background in art direction, did
not have the degree of control over this film that he had
with THE BEAST FROM 20,000 FATHOMS; the special effects
were shot without any imput or supervision from Lourie.

The monster itself is well designed and nicely animated
under O'Brien's supervision by Pete Peterson, but the technical work is compromised by budgetary limitations.   Out of
necessity, some shots of this fictional monster (called a "pale-
osaurus") are used more than once, and although the footage
is sometimes optically cropped or reversed in an effort to
disguise this, the repetition is still apparent.   One shot in

particular, of the monster's foot smashing a car, is repeated
several times.

A few of the miniatures, such as cars falling into a
river when the monster destroys a ferry boat, are poorly
done, but the process photography and miniature settings,
considering the low effects budget (only $20,000!) are quite
adequate. Some of these scenes were so cheaply filmed that
photo cut-outs were used to represent buildings, though stop-
gap measures such as this are surprisingly effective. A live
action mock-up of the behemoth's head, originally designed
to provide fully articulated head and neck movements in order
to save time on animation, was broken before filming. Since
there was no time to repair it before shooting began, it appears onscreen--stiff, lifeless, and unconvincing.

Tragically misused by the film industry in the latter
portion of his career, Willis O'Brien spent his last years toiling on unrealized projects. Sadly, THE GIANT BEHEMOTH
represents O'Brien's last animation work, and, even though
he was hampered by an excruciatingly tight budget, it should
be noted that he brought all the skill and craftsmanship he
could provide to a job that he must have considered thankless.

26. JOURNEY TO THE CENTER OF THE EARTH

20th Century-Fox, 1959

Credits:

Producer: Charles Brackett
Director: Henry Levin
Screenplay: Walter Reisch and Charles Brackett; based on
    the novel by Jules Verne
Camera: Leo Tover
Special Effects: L.B. Abbott, James B. Gordon, and Emil
    Kosa, Jr.
Art Directors: Lyle R. Wheeler, Franz Bachelin, and Herman
    A. Blumenthal
Set Decorators: Walter M. Scott and Joseph Kish
Music: Bernard Hermann; conducted by Lionel Newman
Songs: Sammy Cahn, James Van Heusen, and Robert Burns
Costumes: David Folkes
Sound: Bernard Freericks and Warren E. Delaplain
Editors: Stuart Gilmore and Jack W. Holmes
Makeup: Ben Nye

Cast:

James Mason (Prof. Oliver Lindenbrook)
Arlene Dahl (Carla)
Pat Boone (Alec McEwen)
Diane Baker (Jenny)
Thayer David (Count Saknussemm)
Peter Ronson (Hans)
Robert Adler (Groom)
Alan Napier (Dean)
Alex Finlayson (Prof. Bayle)

Ben Wright (Paisley)
Mary Brady (Kirsty)
Frederick Halliday (Chancellor)
Alan Caillou (Rector)

JOURNEY TO THE CENTER OF THE EARTH is one of
the most successful movie adaptations of a Jules Verne story,
and one of the most entertaining fantasy-adventures ever
filmed. Professor Oliver Lindenbrook (James Mason), discovering a route to the center of the earth, promptly embarks
on an expedition in search of missing explorer Arnie Saknussemm, who had previously descended through the same pas-
sage without returning. Accompanied by his associates Alec
McEwen (Pat Boone), Carla (Arlene Dahl), and Hans (Peter
Ronson), Lindenbrook attempts to reach his goal before his
rival (a relative of Saknussemm's) arrives at the earth's core
first and claims credit for the feat himself.

Although scientifically impossible (the earth's core is
represented as being hollow, with a sea at the center and il-
lumination provided by mineral phosphorescence), the picture
does not seek to convince, only to entertain, and succeeds
admirably in that pursuit. Shot in Cinemascope, the film
makes excellent use of the wide-screen format, offering sweep-
ing panoramic views of subterranean caverns, many of them
filmed on location. The special effects, the miniatures, and
the matte photography, are excellent; a herd of dimetrodons,
represented by lizards with rubber fins shot in slow-motion,
are the best live-action monsters filmed since ONE MILLION
B.C.

The sets are cheerfully unrealistic, brightly colored
and surprisingly varied. Glittering mineral veins sparkle in
the cavern walls and giant mushrooms sprout from the su
terranean loam, while the crumbling remnants of legendary
Atlantis (concealing an unexpected saurian menace) and the
subterranean dimetrodon-infested beach are all somehow enhanced by the obvious studio origin of the sets.

Director Henry Levin handles the actors well and contributes a few imaginative camera set-ups. When a reptilian
monster ensnares James Mason with its serpentine tongue,
there is a bizarre angle showing Mason struggling, shot from
inside the creature's mouth! Pleasantly light-hearted in tone

and refreshingly unpretentious in design, with a few songs
even thrown in for good measure, this big-budget picture
benefits from all the technical finesse a major studio is capa-
ble of and the extreme length (132 minutes) passes more
quickly than one would expect. Only the inordinate amount
of footage expended on Pat Boone (who was quite popular at
the time and acquits himself surprisingly well) mars the film's
pacing. In compensation, Thayer David provides some enjoyably slimy villainy and James Mason, as he wanders through
the garish subterranean forests of giant mushrooms and the
ruined temples of Atlantis, reminds the viewer that the presence of a first-rate actor in this sort of material is worth
more than all the special effects in the world.

In 1978, JOURNEY TO THE CENTER OF THE EARTH
was ineptly remade as WHERE TIME BEGAN, with a predic-
table array of immobile mechanical dinosaur mock-ups.

[Opposite:] JOURNEY TO THE CENTER OF THE EARTH:
In this frame enlargement, a hungry dimetrodon ogles Arlene
Dahl. (Photo courtesy of George Turner.)

27. DINOSAURUS

Universal, 1960

Credits:

Producer: Jack H. Harris
Director: Irvin S. Yeaworth, Jr.
Screenplay: Jean Yeaworth and Dan E. Weisburd
Camera: Stanley Cortez
Special Effects: Tim Barr, Wah Chang, and Gene Warren
Art Director: Jack Senter
Assistant Directors: Paul Stader and Herbert Mendelson
Associate Producer: Irvin S. Yeaworth, Jr.
Music: Ronald Stein
Sound: Jack Conall, Jack Wheeler, and Vic Appel
Editor: John A. Bushelman
Set Decorator: Herman Schoenbrun
Makeup: Don Cash

Cast:

Ward Ramsey (Bart Thompson)
Kristina Hanson (Betty Piper)
Paul Lukather (Chuck)
Gregg Martell (Neanderthal)
Alan Roberts (Julio)
Fred Engleberg (Mike Hacker)
Wayne C. Tredway (Dumpy)
James Logan (O'Leary)
Luci Blain (Chica)
Jack Younger (Jasper)
Howard Dayton (Mousey)

DINOSAURUS: An animated brontosaurus carries a juvenile passenger, also an animated figure.

Straightforwardly juvenile in concept, DINOSAURUS relates the misadventures of a brontosaurus and tyrannosaurus, as well as a Neanderthal man, the three of which are revived by lightning after they are unearthed by a construction crew. By the film's conclusion a young boy befriends the brontosaurus, the Neanderthal man encounters the dubious pleasures of civilization when he invades a home during a low-comedy sequence, and the tyrannosaurus engages a construction crane in battle.

This film is inoffensively silly without being condescending and offers some well-constructed stop-motion dinosaurs built by Marcel Delgado of KING KONG. Although these dinosaurs are hastily and crudely animated, the film does not seek to convince on any level, and the cartoonish nature of the monsters is somewhat appropriate under the circumstances.

Shot in color by the great cinematographer Stanley
Cortez, who filmed THE MAGNIFICENT AMBERSONS (1942)
for Orson Welles, DINOSAURUS is a type of movie that has
become increasingly rare: good, solid, and thoroughly honest
children's entertainment.

28. GORGO

MGM, 1960

Credits:

Producer: Wilfred Eades
Director: Eugene Lourie
Screenplay: John Loring and Daniel Hyatt
Camera: F.A. Young
Special Effects: Tom Howard
Art Director: Elliott Scott
Music: Angelo Lavagnino
Editor: Eric Boyd-Perkins
Assistant Director: Douglas Hermes

Cast:

Bill Travers (Joe)
William Sylvester (Sam)
Vincent Winter (Sean)
Christopher Rhodes (McCartin)
Joseph O'Connor (Prof. Hendricks)
Martin Benson (Dorkin)
Basil Dignam (Admiral)
Bruce Seton (Prof. Flaherty)
Maurice Kauffman (radio reporter)
Howard Lang (1st Colonel)
Thomas Duggan (1st naval officer)
Dervis Ward (bosun)
Barry Keegan (mate)

The man-in-a-costume approach to the presentation of

GORGO: The monster destroys a bathysphere.

giant screen monsters has always been the least successful
method employed by producers, and, unfortunately, it is the
method used most frequently by low-budget filmmakers. Although the "advantages" of stuffing a man in a dinosaur costume (in other words, effects scenes that can be filmed
cheaply and simply without depending on time-consuming
stop-motion animation) are understandably appealing to low-
budget producers, who must shoot their films quickly in order
to turn an immediate profit, the disadvantages are painfully
obvious and are on display for all to see in films like UN-
KNOWN ISLAND and THE LAND UNKNOWN.

There are, however, exceptions to every rule, and
GORGO is one such exception, proving that costumed monsters can work, and work very well in the bargain. The
problem with most such attempts at monster costumes is that
the human form cannot, no matter how cleverly it is concealed,
approximate the shape and physique of, for instance, a tyrannosaurus, as the costumed tyrannosaur in THE LAND UN-
KNOWN proves. For GORGO (short for the Gorgon of Greek
mythology, whose fearsome gaze turned its victims to stone)
the special effects technicians designed a costume that roughly
approximates the human form, and the onscreen monster looks
alive and relatively convincing as a result.

Directed by Eugene Lourie, who also directed THE
BEAST FROM 20,000 FATHOMS and THE GIANT BEHEMOTH,
GORGO is perhaps the best picture of the three, at least in
terms of plot. Although a virtual retread of KING KONG
(an ambitious showman plans to exhibit Gorgo for profit),
the script is enlivened by a few ingenious twists (the huge
monster captured is revealed to be a mere infant, with the
much larger mother on her way to claim the offspring), and
an ending that had been used for THE LOST WORLD (1925),
but had seen little service in the years since: the two monsters are not destroyed, but simply return peacefully to the
sea after they have ravaged London.

Although slightly marred by some arbitrary changes in
the script made over Lourie's objections (particularly the in-
sertion of scenes depicting a military offensive against the
monster, which Lourie felt were ridiculous since no living
animal--no matter how large--could survive the massive display of firepower shown onscreen), as well as some crude and
badly done matte photography, the picture is at least different

from others of its type, offering a tranquil (and strangely
appropriate) musical score and all the technical finesse that
a studio like M-G-M could provide. Unlike many of his low-
budget contemporaries, Eugene Lourie cared about his work,
and GORGO, his most expensive monster film, is a fine tribute
to his efforts.

29. REPTILICUS

American-International, 1962

Credits:

Producer: Sidney Pink
Director: Sidney Pink
Screenplay: Ib Melchior and Sidney Pink
Camera: Aage Wiltrup
Music: Sven Gyldmark
Editor: Svend Mehling

Cast:

Carl Ottosen (Mark Grayson)
Ann Smyrner (Lise Martens)
Mimi Heinrich (Karen Martens)
Asbjorn Andersen (Prof. Martens)
Marla Behrens (Connie Miller)
Bent Mejding (Svend Viltofft)
Poul Wildaker (Dr. Dalby)
Dirk Passer (Dirk Mikkelsen)
Ole Wisborg (Capt. Brandt)

This low-budget Danish production, released in English-dubbed form by American-International, is undoubtedly one of the worst pictures of its type ever made, and, along with a handful of others like it such as KING DINOSAUR, is is included here only as a clinical example of exactly how bad such a film can be. They certainly don't come any worse, or more disappointing for that matter, than REPTILICUS. Whereas some films may be so inept that they are inintentionally

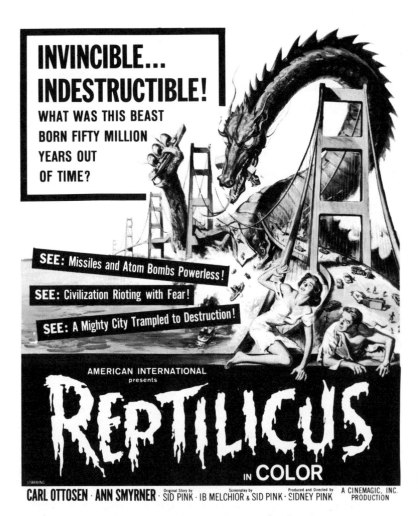

REPTILICUS: The promotional ads promised a lot.

amusing, REPTILICUS fails to grant its audience even that
slight virtue.

The title fiend is inadvertently unleashed when a construction crew digging a well excavates the bloody frozen
tail of a prehistoric reptile, and it is discovered that this
grisly remnant has the ability to regenerate its own cells.
As the severed tail thaws, a complete monster of immense
size is reformed and promptly embarks on the traditional as-
sault against civilization (why these revived prehistoric
beasts don't simply retreat to an uninhabited area and live
in placid solitude is anyone's guess). The army is stymied,
having determined that if heavy artillery is used against
Reptilicus and the monster is blown to bits, each piece of the
remains will form into a new animal (not that anyone in the
audience cared by this point).

Advertising material promoting REPTILICUS featured
impressive artwork vividly depicting the fearsome title monster

REPTILICUS: The monster in the film hardly fulfilled the
promise of the ads.

destroying a bridge while a scantily clad maiden cowered in the foreground. Unfortunately for the paying audience, the lurid posters outside the theatre promised far more, and were definitely more entertaining, than the miserable film shown onscreen.

The special effects in REPTILICUS are inexcusably pathetic. The serpentine monster (a fictional species) is represented by a poorly controlled marionette, so restricted in its movements that its mouth never closes and remains permanently agape in a rigid sneer. This sad little puppet thrashes about ineffectively in miniature sets, leering sheepishly from between badly scaled miniature buildings and periodically expectorating nauseous, corrosive green bile (added to the scenes via obvious cartoon animation) at the fleeing populace. The monster also had the power of flight in the original foreign version, but these views of Reptilicus sailing through the air were so incompetent that this footage was deleted from domestic prints by none-too-discriminating American-International.

As is often the case with foreign movies released in America, the dubbing is abominable; but far more damaging to the film is its limp editing. The picture might not have been improved by cutting, but it certainly would have moved faster and would have been easier to watch if American-International had at least tightened up the editing by trimming a scene here and there and shortening the excruciating 90-minute running time.

So bad that clips from it were often used as comic gags on The Monkees television series, REPTILICUS, if nothing else, surely gave its audience a painful and memorable lesson concerning truth in advertising.

30. JOURNEY TO THE BEGINNING OF TIME

New Trends Associates, 1966

Credits:

Producer: William Cayton
Director: Karel Zeman
Screenplay: William Cayton and Karel Zeman
Additional Dialogue: Fred Ladd
Camera: Anthony Huston
Music: E.F. Burian
Technical Advisor: Dr. Edwin H. Colbert

Cast:

James Lukas (Doc)
Peter Hermann (Tony)
Charles Goldsmith (Ben)
Victor Betral (Joe)

Czech director Karel Zeman's JOURNEY TO THE BE-
GINNING OF TIME (CESTA DO PRAVEKU) is almost unique
in its attempt to blend education with entertainment.   The
plot concerns four youths who, during a visit to the American Museum of Natural History in New York, are mesmerized
by the hypnotic gaze of an Indian medicine man sculpture.
Enjoying a rowboat ride after they have left the museum,
they follow the river through an ominous rocky overpass.
When the boat emerges on the other side they find themselves
lost and traveling down and unknown river.

The weather begins to grow colder, and eventually they

JOURNEY TO THE BEGINNING OF TIME: The young explorers
in a prehistoric swamp.

see animals that have been extinct since the Ice Age. They
encounter a woolly mammoth, and Doc, the leader of the
group, theorizes that they are somehow traveling back into
time. A paleontology buff, he takes copious notes as they
progress on their journey. As the boys travel down the
mystical river, the world's evolutionary history unfolds before them, in reverse. They see a smilodon (saber-toothed
tiger) loping across the plains in search of prey. Entering
the Mesozoic Era they witness a struggle to the death between
a ceratosaurus and a stegosaurus. A pterodactyl buzzes
their rowboat like a dive bomber, and they see a placid
brontosaurus grazing in the marsh. During all of these encounters with extinct life forms, Doc offers his friends--and
the audience--information on each of the animals they see,
such as the scientific names, physical dimensions, and eating
habits of each.

Backward they travel, into the Devonian Age, and even farther into the world's distant formative stages until, in a somewhat audacious sequence, they stand at the very edge of Creation surrounded by abstract sounds and light patterns, with Doc quoting from the book of Genesis. At the film's conclusion, the boys suddenly awaken in the American Museum of Natural History, under the gaze of the Indian medicine man's statue, wondering if their fantastic experience had been a dream, or reality.

Originally released in 1954 in Europe, JOURNEY TO THE BEGINNING OF TIME was dubbed into English and distributed in the United States in 1966. Oddly, the picture was also re-edited into a multichapter serial (with each installment running about five minutes) and distributed to television by National Educational Television. The film is something of a technical milestone since it is the first live-action feature to use stop-motion animation in color.

JOURNEY TO THE BEGINNING OF TIME: An animated woolly mammoth.

Director Karel Zeman also filmed THE FABULOUS WORLD OF JULES VERNE (1961), a diverting fantasy combining live action and animation in such a way that the scenes are given the appearance of living Victorian engravings. Zeman's puppet animation in JOURNEY TO THE BEGINNING OF TIME is generally smooth, although his techniques for combining his models with live actors are rudimentary. In a typical scene, instead of using rear projection or traveling mattes, Zeman instead directs his actors to point at an off-screen monster, the camera then executes a fast, violent "swish" pan in that direction, with Zeman continuing the pan in a separate shot onto the miniature set, with a simple cut on the blurred pan action joining the two shots. The cuts are still readily apparent, but even though the technique is crude, it is serviceable. There are a few stationary mattes combining the actors and puppets, but for the most part the models and live actors do not interact. Possibly, the fact that this was the first movie of its type shot in color imposed technical limitations, but Zeman did manage to surmount these difficulties in some ingenious ways. After the stegosaurus versus ceratosaurus battle, Doc and his friends decide to inspect the dead stegosaurus. Taking its measurements, the boys actually walk on the animal's back, between the dorsal plates. This startling shot was actually realized through the simple use of forced perspective; the puppet was suspended close to the camera while the actors were actually walking on a much larger parallel structure in the distance. Although hampered by somewhat murky and grainy color, dull editing, and direction that is at times curiously listless, JOURNEY TO THE BEGINNING OF TIME is still an entertaining and well-crafted picture.

A good pictorialist director would have really been able to work wonders with this material, but Karel Zeman certainly did well enough, managing to avoid most of the clichés usually found in movies dealing with prehistory and offering his audience a little scientific education in the bargain.

Warner Bros., 1969

Credits:

Producer: Charles H. Schneer
Director: James O'Connolly
Screenplay: William E. Bast and Julian More
Camera: Erwin Hillier
Special Effects: Ray Harryhausen
Music: Jerome Moross
Sound: Malcolm Stewart
Editor: Henry Richardson
Associate Producer: Ray Harryhausen

Cast:

James Franciscus (Tuck)
Gila Colan (T.J.)
Richard Carlson (Champ)
Laurece Naismith (Professor Bromley)
Freda Jackson (Tia Zorina)
Gustavo Rojo (Carlos)
Dennis Kilbane (Rowdy)
Mario De Barros (Bean)
Curtis Arden (Lope)

Based on an unfilmed Willis O'Brien concept from the 1940s, THE VALLEY OF GWANGI was practically thrown away when it was released by Warner Bros. in 1969. At this time, when social commentary and trendy rebellion were the then-fashionable selling points of many American films, confused

THE VALLEY OF GWANGI: The allosaurus attacks a styracosaurus, as rear-projected cowboys watch.

Hollywood studios had little faith in the sort of straightforward, unpretentious adventure pictures Ray Harryhausen
and Charles Schneer were still making. As a result of the
poor distribution and lack of promotion that THE VALLEY OF
GWANGI received, the film was not very profitable at the
box-office, and Harryhausen was seriously considering re-
tiring over the incident, although he and Schneer later
bounced back with the hugely successful THE GOLDEN VOY-
AGE OF SINBAD (1974).

        THE VALLEY OF GWANGI concerns the discovery of an
allosaurus (known as "Gwangi" to the local peasants) in a
hidden Mexican valley. The monster is captured and put on
display in a wild west show from which it escapes, terrorizing
the local town before finally perishing when it is trapped in
a burning church. The allosaurus, as well as the other prehistoric inhabitants of the valley (a pteranodon, an eohippus,
a styracosaurus, and an ornithomimus), as well as a circus
elephant, are all extremely well animated by Harryhausen, but
the film lacks energy and strong direction and is basically
just a tired reworking of KING KONG.

THE VALLEY OF GWANGI: An original promotional ad.

The picture is certainly acceptable children's fare, but because Warner Bros. released it on a double-bill with a sex-oriented film, THE VALLEY OF GWANGI failed to attract an appropriately juvenile audience. Although otherwise a mediocre picture, THE VALLEY OF GWANGI succeeds as a demonstration of Ray Harryhausen's craftsmanship and as yet another example of the unlimited possibilities available to film-makers through stop-motion animation.

Warner Bros., 1970

Credits:

Producer: Aida Young
Director: Val Guest
Screenplay: Val Guest; treatment by J.B. Ballard
Camera: Dick Bush and Johnny Cabrera
Special Effects: Jim Danforth, Allan Bryce, Roger Dicken,
    and Brian Johncock
Art Director: John Blezard
Music: Mario Nascimbene
Sound: Kevin Sutton
Editor: Peter Curran
Costumes: Carl Toms

Cast:

Victoria Vetri (Sanna)
Robin Hawdon (Tara)
Patrick Holt (Ammon)
Patrick Allen (Kingsor)
Drewe Henley (Khaku)
Magda Konopka (Ulido)
Sean Caffrey (Kane)
Imogen Hassall (Ayak)
Maria O'Brien (Omah)
Jan Rossini (Rock girl)
Connie Tilton (Sand mother)
Maggie Lynton (Rock mother)
Carol-Anne Hawkins (Yanni)
Jimmy Lodge (fisherman)

WHEN DINOSAURS RULED THE EARTH: A chasmosaurus
pursues a caveman.

Ray Ford (hunter)
Billy Cornelius (hunter)

    WHEN DINOSAURS RULED THE EARTH, an otherwise
negligible retread of ONE MILLION B.C., features some of
the finest stop-motion animation ever seen, courtesy of Jim
Danforth.   For this film Danforth, who has contributed effects to JACK THE GIANT KILLER (1962) and THE SEVEN
FACES OF DR. LAO (1964), devised a method for eliminating
the strobing inherent in all stop-motion animation.   Simply
explained, this involved shooting the animated models through
a sheet of glass and at predetermined intervals producing an
artificial blur on the action by smearing vaseline on the appropriate glass area.   This softened the heightened clarity
of the animation, producing much more realistic action.   Although the technique is highly successful (the animation is

so smooth that the dinosaurs look uncannily alive in many
scenes), Danforth's meticulous efforts were so time-consuming
that the effects for this picture took 17 months to complete.
The various monsters--a plesiosaur, a ramphorynchus, a
chasmosaurus (this model was animated by David Allen), and
a fictional giant saurian that befriends a voluptuous cave
girl--are all impeccably designed and constructed.

The picture does not take itself too seriously, and,
despite the technical virtuosity and the spectacular visuals
on display, it is a remarkably unpretentious film. Deservedly,
Jim Danforth was an Academy Award nominee for his commendable work on WHEN DINOSAURS RULED THE EARTH,
and predictably, lost the Oscar to the more popular (but
technically inferior) Disney film BEDKNOBS AND BROOM-
STICKS.

33. THE LAND THAT TIME FORGOT

American-International, 1975

Credits:

Director: Kevin Connor
Screenplay: James Cawthorne and Michael Moorcock; based
    on the novel by Edgar Rice Burroughs
Camera: Alan Hume and Charles Staffel
Special Effects: Derek Meddings and Roger Dicken
Production Design: Maurice Carter
Music: Douglas Gamley
Makeup: Tom Smith

Cast:

Doug McClure (Bowen Tyler)
Susan Penhaligon (Lisa Clayton)
John McEnery (Capt. Von Schoevorts)
Anthony Ainley (Lt. Diets)
Keith Barron (Bradley)
Godfrey James (Borg)
Bobby Farr (Ahm)
Declan Mulholland (Olson)
Ben Howard (Benson)
Colin Farrell (Whitely)
Roy Holder (Plesser)
Andrew McCulloch (Sinclair)
Grahame Mallard (Deusett)
Brian Hall (Schwartz)
Peter Sproule (Hindle)
Ron Pember (Jones)
Andrew Lodge (Reuther)

Stanley McGeagh (Hiller)
Steve James (1st sto-lu)

Edgar Rice Burroughs, the prolific and hugely successful writer who created Tarzan for a pulp magazine in 1912,
also penned a number of exotic and romantic adventure tales
with a prehistoric setting, the most famous of which were
his Pellucidar series, set in a mythical land of that name
located in the center of the earth and inhabited by creatures
from the dawn of time.

Hollywood producers were quick to successfully exploit
Burroughs' popular Tarzan character almost from the beginning (the first Tarzan film was released in 1918, the most
recent in 1984). However, his "prehistoric" novels, despite
their obvious potential, were always strangely neglected by
filmmakers, probably because the necessary special effects
would complicate any such adaptation, both financially and
technically.

THE LAND THAT TIME FORGOT: A plesiosaur attacks a
German U-boat.

Perhaps the ideal interpreters of these Burroughs ad-
ventures would have been the KING KONG creative team of
Cooper, Schoedsack, and O'Brien, and Cooper's 1935 production of SHE certainly demonstrates that such a collaboration
would have been effective with this type of material.   Even
Charles Schneer and Ray Harryhausen could have done jus-
tice to the Burroughs stories.   If Harryhausen could have
filmed one of the Pellucidar novels with the right script and
actors, he could possibly have created a worthy successor
to KING KONG.   Sadly, none of this ever came to pass, and
when the Burroughs prehistoric stories finally did reach the
screen, they appeared in a trilogy of films under the American-
International logo, all three of them featuring an inadequate
Doug McClure in the lead role.

First in release was THE LAND THAT TIME FORGOT
in 1975, a World War I story marooning a German U-boat crew
and their prisoners in a hidden prehistoric land at the North
Pole.   The various dinosaurs involved were represented either
by life-sized mock-ups or by live-action puppets, which, for
obvious reasons, are only seen from the midriff up.   These
saurian concoctions range from marginally acceptable (a
plesiosaurus mock-up) to painfully inadequate (a pair of
tyrannosaurus puppets, lifelessly snapping their jaws like
toy alligators from behind concealing shrubbery).

Although hardly destined for classic status, THE LAND
THAT TIME FORGOT was adequate entertainment, thankfully
(and surprisingly, in 1975) straightforward and generally
serious in tone.   The second film, AT THE EARTH'S CORE
(1976), was decidedly tongue-in-cheek, taking place in Burroughs' subterranean Pellucidar and presenting Doug Mc-
Clure as Burroughs' hero David Innes.   McClure offers a
rather smug and condescending performance, apparently believing himself superior to the project, and the film is even
cheaper and the special effects even more unconvincing than
the previous movie.   The third offering, THE PEOPLE THAT
TIME FORGOT (1977), was the lowest point in an already
ignominious series.   A sequel to THE LAND THAT TIME FOR-
GOT, THE PEOPLE THAT TIME FORGOT featured Patrick
Wayne in the lead with Doug McClure again cast in a reprise
of his role in the first picture.   In this movie, the cheapest
of the three, the direction is sluggish (Kevin Connor directed
all three films) and the special effects are depressingly inept,
with a stegosaurus, for instance, represented by a life-sized

mock-up so inert that it seems Wayne and his companions
have stumbled upon an abandoned parade float.

Thankfully, THE PEOPLE THAT TIME FORGOT proved
to be the last installment in this series. While there have
been many failures and many regretfully unrealized projects
in film history, Hollywood's inability to provide successful
movie versions of stories that are among Edgar Rice Burroughs' most vivid and romantic must surely rank as one of
the major cinematic disappointments, at least for aficionados
of fantasy and adventure in film. The American-International
Burroughs trilogy only serves to intensify that disappointment.

34. SINBAD AND THE EYE OF THE TIGER

Columbia, 1977

Credits:

Producer: Charles H. Schneer
Director: Sam Wanamaker
Screenplay: Beverly Cross; story by Ray Harryhausen and
    Beverly Cross
Camera: Ted Moore
Special Effects: Ray Harryhausen
Music: Roy Budd
Sound: George Stephenson
Costumes: Cynthia Tingey
Art Directors: Fred Carter and Fernando Gonzales
Production Design: Geoffrey Drake
Editor: Roy Watts
Makeup: Colin Arthur
Associate Producer: Ray Harryhausen

Cast:

Patrick Wayne (Sinbad)
Taryn Power (Dione)
Jane Seymour (Farah)
Margaret Whiting (Zenobia)
Patrick Troughton (Melanthius)
Kurt Christian (Rafi)

[Opposite:] SINBAD AND THE EYE OF THE TIGER: The
troglodyte battles a smilodon.

Nadim Sawaiha (Hassan)
Salami Coker (Maroof)
Bruno Barnabe (Balsora)
David Stern (Aboo-Seer)

In 1977, the release of Ray Harryhausen's SINBAD
AND THE EYE OF THE TIGER coincided with the release of
STAR WARS, and, unfortunately, the Harryhausen picture
suffered by comparison. Although hailed as a technical advance at the time, the special effects in STAR WARS were
not all that revolutionary. Most of them, in fact, were
traditional in concept and execution, but what really put the
film over was its rapid-fire editing. STAR WARS (like KING
KONG) was edited for maximum impact with its makers stead-
fastly refusing to be awestruck by their own technical virtuosity.

Sadly, the opposite has always been the main drawback
with Ray Harryhausen's movies. Far too many of them lurch
from special effect to special effect, with the usually unin-
volving actors periodically stopping in their tracks so that
Harryhausen can trot out his undeniably impressive bag of
tricks at regular intervals. As fascinating as Harryhausen's
animation can be, such technical virtuosity cannot support a
film alone, and as a result, Harryhausen's pictures often de-
generate into mere special-effects demonstration reels. Harryhausen, a precise and dedicated technician, deserves better,
and so does his audience.

This Sinbad adventure, the third Harryhausen movie
featuring the character after THE SEVENTH VOYAGE OF
SINBAD (1958) and THE GOLDEN VOYAGE OF SINBAD (1974)
is a pretty turgid affair, only somewhat enlivened by Sinbad's encounters with a few prehistoric monsters in addition
to the usual parade of mythical creatures. A fictional sub-
human troglodyte, a giant walrus, and a saber-toothed tiger
are all well constructed and smoothly animated, but the plot
is thin (a prince has been magically transformed into a baboon, and Sinbad attempts to cure him), with the actors only
adequate. Lovely Jane Seymour provides the only live-action
diversions.

Unlike his mentor, Willis O'Brien, Ray Harryhausen,
serving as his own associate producer, has managed to insure

financial success for himself and gain a measure of creative control over his work in the bargain. Paradoxically, also unlike O'Brien, the promise of his considerable talent has remained largely unfilled.

35. CAVEMAN

Credits:

Producers: Lawrence Turman and David Foster
Director: Carl Gottlieb
Screenplay: Rudy de Luca and Carl Gottlieb
Camera: Alan Hume
Special Effects: David Allen, Jim Aupperle, Randall William
    Cook, Spencer Gill, Pete Kleinow, David Stipes, and Laine
    Liska
Opticals: Howard A. Anderson Co.
Matte Artists: Dan Curry, Rocco Gioffre, and Jena Holman
Music: Lalo Schifrin
Sound: Claude Hitchcock
Editor: Gene Fowler
Mechanical Effects: Roy Arbogast

Cast:

Ringo Starr (Atouk)
Barbara Bach (Lana)
Jack Gilford (Gog)
Shelly Long (Tala)
Dennis Quaid (Lar)
John Metuszak (Tonda)
Cork Hubbert (Ta)
Mark King (Ruck)
Paco Morayta (Flok)
Evan Kim (Nook)
Ed Greenberg (Kalta)
Carl Lumbly (Bork)

Jack Scalici (Folg)
Erica Carlson (Folg's mate)
Sara Lopez Sierra (Folg's daughter)

CAVEMAN is a unique prehistoric comedy playing its animated dinosaurs for laughs, but while the idea of spoofing the ONE MILLION B.C. type of film may have more validity than simply churning out another weary retread of the same concept, the movie falls short of its considerable possibilities. One can imagine a good visual comedian like Buster Keaton or Stan Laurel handling such material, and indeed, a Laurel and Hardy two-reel silent "prehistoric comedy," FLYING ELEPHANTS (1927), did present the team in this setting (without monsters). Keaton, too, featured a "prehistoric" sequence in his feature-length comedy THE THREE AGES (1923) as stone-age Buster cavorted with a stop-motion brontosaurus in a brief shot.

As with most 1970s and 1980s film comedy, the humor in CAVEMAN is broad, overstated, and frequently scatological in nature, with the performers mugging in the worst Jerry Lewis tradition. The film is just not as funny as it could and should be, although the unique monsters, designed with crossed eyes and other comic features, are amusing, with a duplicate of Harryhausen's rhedosaurus from THE BEAST FROM 20,000 FATHOMS baying at the moon as an inside joke. The composite photography and the animation of these slapstick monsters are clean and uniformly excellent. Originally, Jim Danforth was to handle the animation. After initially declining, he did supervise the effects with David Allen assisting, although Danforth eventually left the production before completion. David Allen recalls:

> The picture was ready for filming, and we went to Mexico where it was shot, and at that time I joined the production full-time. I think I worked on it about a year. About four or five months from the end of the picture Jim left to work with Ray Harryhausen in England on CLASH OF THE TITANS, so from that point I took over his duties, and Pete Kleinow, Randy Cook and I finished it.

Allen recalls that the comic dinosaurs were mostly director Carl Gottlieb's idea.

He had it in his mind to play these dinosaurs for
laughs. The storyboards were worked out pretty
carefully for the basic ideas, and Randy Cook and
Pete Kleinow did almost all of that gag animation,
and I think they did a very good job with it. It
required a different type of thinking than we generally employ when we animate monsters.

Although CAVEMAN is a failure as a movie, the excellent technical work succeeds admirably. The film's amusing
dinosaurs make the picture worthwhile, further demostrating
the infinite possibilities of stop-motion animation.

36. Q

UFD, 1982

Credits:

Producer: Larry Cohen
Director: Larry Cohen
Screenplay: Larry Cohen
Camera: Fred Murphy
Special Effects: David Allen, Randy Cook, and Peter Kuran
Model Construction: Roger Dicken, Dennis Gordon, Aiko,
    and Deed Rossiter
Music: Robert O. Ragland
Sound: Jeff Hayes
Makeup: Dennis Enger
Stunt Co-ordinator: Peter Hock

Cast:

Michael Moriarty (Jimmy Quinn)
Candy Clark (Joan)
David Carradine (Shepard)
Richard Roundtree (Powell)
James Dixon (Murray)
Malachy McCourt (Commissioner)
Fred J. Scollay (Fletcher)
Peter Hock (Clifford)
Ron Cey (Detective Hoberman)
Mary Louise Weller (Mrs. Pauley)
Bruce Carradine (victim)
Bobbi Burns (sunbather)

Like CAVEMAN (1981), Q is not a very good film. It is, frankly, exploitation trash, but thoroughly honest about its status and occasionally enjoyable. Also like CAVEMAN, it at least represents an attempt to weave a different pattern from threadbare materials. The Mexican gos Quetzalcoatl, which in different form had served mad scientist George Zucco well in THE FLYING SERPENT (1946), appears in New York, attacking and killing several people. The film unconvincingly explains that by gliding in alignment with the mid-day sun, the giant flying reptile is able to pounce on its hapless victims unseen. Jimmy Quinn, an inept con man, discovers the monster's nest in the cone of the Chrysler building and blackmails the city government for money in exchange for this information. In the film's conclusion, a heavily armed N.Y.P.D. team battles and defeats the monster atop the building, in a reworking of King Kong's demise.

Although the picture is cynical and occasionally funny, the results are uneven. The presentation of Michael Moriarty's Jimmy Quinn character as the nominal "hero" is only partially successful; he is such a sour loser that it is difficult to sympathize with him. David Carradine, always a wooden and inexpressive actor, is well-cast as a jaundiced detective; Candy Clark is attractive as Moriarty's girlfriend. The use of stop-motion animation is surprising in a picture of this nature, and works very well, although use of the process was apparently not intended at the outset and the technical quality is flawed as a result.

Animator David Allen recalls:

> It was a film of a kind that I have had experience with in the past, where the film has basically already been made, and then you come in later and kind of figure out how to stick your effects in, which is not the best way to work.
>
> Steve Neil, who had done make-up effects for Larry Cohen in a couple of other films was a good friend of Randy Cook's, and of mine, and turned Randy on to the project when Cohen announced that he would need some kind of an effect to create the bird. Then Randy, after making a deal with Cohen to design the creature, came to me, sort of secondarily, because he needed facilities and equipment, which he didn't own, to photograph the

creature, also, I'm sure he felt he needed another animator to share the work load, so the two of us animated the show. I had Dennis Gordon with me to do the miniatures that were necessary.

I think when Cohen began that picture, he didn't have animation in mind. He had a large prop head and feet made in New York, and tried to make the film with just those props, but when they cut everything together, they realized that they had just not delivered the goods for the audience. Larry had seen ALIEN (1979), and said he felt the reason the film succeeded was because you hardly ever saw the monster, and he wanted to duplicate that, to just have a flash of a beak or claw, and to have virtually no explicit shots of the entire creature in the picture.

Well, we thought about that and didn't say too much, but it seemed to us that the differences between ALIEN and this picture were considerable, to say the least. ALIEN took place in a closed ship, a claustrophobic environment, and here was a thing that was supposed to be flying in mid-day over Manhattan, so I think we kind of took it upon ourselves to open the film up in that respect and show the creature much more clearly than Larry had ever originally intended. We believed that when he saw the stuff he would like it and want more, and that is in fact what happened. We kind of opened his eyes to the possibilities of animation.

Allen's shooting facilities were limited and the schedule was rushed, with some of the process photography suffering as a result; the projected background plates are particularly weak in a couple of shots. "Some were totally made-up shots from old slides and leftover trims from the editor's bin," Allen recalls. The miniature of Quetzalcoatl was scaled for the limited facilities. The wingspan was only 14 inches, and the head was only an inch long, although a larger head and neck were used for a couple of shots.

Q may not be a great film, but it is, at least, an amusing diversion from the typical monster, and a tribute to the dedication and ingenuity of David Allen and his crew.

37. BABY

Credits:

Producer: Roger Spottiswoode
Director: B.W.L. Norton
Screenplay: Clifford Green and Ellen Green
Camera: John Alcott
Special Effects: Philip Meador, Roland Tantini, and Isidoro Raponi
Art Director: John S. Mansbridge
Matte Artist: Michael Lloyd
Music: Jerry Goldsmith
Sound: Kirk Francis and Shawn Murphy

Cast:

William Katt (George Loomis)
Sean Young (Susan Matthews-Loomis)
Patrick McGoohan (Dr. Eric Kiviat)
Julian Fellowes (Nigel Jenkins)
Kyalo Mativo (Cephu)
Hugh Quarshie (Kenge Obe)
Olu Jacobs (Colonel Nsogbu)
Eddie Tagoe (Sgt. Gambwe)
Edward Hardwicke (Dr. Pierre Dubois)
Julian Curry (Etienne)
Alexis Meless (guide)

BABY, produced by the Disney studio and released through its subsidiary Touchstone Films, provides a memor-

able lesson in how not to make a monster picture. The story
concerns the discovery of a living brontosaurus and its offspring in the jungle, and the efforts of a young scientist
and his wife to prevent a big-game hunter from killing the
dinosaur. Although filmed on a sizable budget, with exten-
sive location shooting, the movie ultimately provides no more
entertainment value than low-budget exploitation fare like
UNTAMED WOMEN, despite a novel plot.

The brontosaurs are badly represented by mechanical
mock-ups and by actors in costumes walking in the manner
of a vaudeville horse; shots of the animals in motion are em-
barrassingly inept and are kept to a minimum. The matte
photography is acceptable, but when the picture's central
concept--the dinosaurs--are so unbelievable, their features
marred by cute anthropomorphic qualities, necessary credibility is irretrievably lost.

In terms of money expended (if not onscreen results),
BABY is one of the most expensive films of its type ever
made. Inevitably, it became yet another casualty in the long
line of big-budget box-office duds produced by Hollywood in
the 1970s and 1980s era of mass-produced, corporate film-
making.

In recent decades, the Disney organization, with its
bland "family" pictures and immense amusement parks, has
been more of public-relations firm than a film-making entity.
Movies like BABY are a potent reminder of how sadly dis-
tanced the studio has become from the Hollywood mainstream.

Live-action feature-length films depicting prehistoric animals.
The films are listed in chronological order of U.S. release.
Films not discussed in this volume are indicated by an asterisk (*) after the entry.

THE THREE AGES (1923)
THE LOST WORLD (1925)
FIG LEAVES (1926)*
THE SAVAGE (1926)*
KING KONG (1933)
SON OF KONG (1933)
ONE MILLION B.C. (1940)
THE FLYING SERPENT (1946)
UNKNOWN ISLAND (1948)
THE LOST VOLCANO (1950)*
PREHISTORIC WOMEN (1950)*
TWO LOST WORLDS (1950)*
JUNGLE MANHUNT (1951)*
THE JUNGLE (1952)
THE LOST CONTINENT (1952)
THE BEAST FROM 20,000 FATHOMS (1953)
ROBOT MONSTER (1953)*
THE CREATURE FROM THE BLACK LAGOON (1954)
IT CAME FROM BENEATH THE SEA (1955)
THE ANIMAL WORLD (1956)
THE BEAST OF HOLLOW MOUNTAIN (1956)
THE SHE-CREATURE (1956)
THE BLACK SCORPION (1957)
THE DEADLY MANTIS (1957)
THE GIANT CLAW (1957)
THE LAND UNKNOWN (1957)
THE MONSTER THAT CHALLENGED THE WORLD (1957)

MONSTER ON THE CAMPUS (1958)*
TEENAGE CAVEMAN (1958)*
THE GIANT BEHEMOTH (1959)
JOURNEY TO THE CENTER OF THE EARTH (1959)
DINOSAURUS (1960)
THE LOST WORLD (1960)
MYSTERIOUS ISLAND (1961)*
VALLEY OF THE DRAGONS (1961)
REPTILICUS (1962)
JOURNEY TO THE BEGINNING OF TIME (1966)
ONE MILLION YEARS B.C. (1966)
JOURNEY TO THE CENTER OF TIME (1967)*
THE VALLEY OF GWANGI (1969)
THE MIGHTY GORGA (1970)*
TROG (1970)
VAMPIRE MEN OF THE LOST PLANET (1970)
WHEN DINOSAURS RULED THE EARTH (1970)
THE LAND THAT TIME FORGOT (1975)
AT THE EARTH'S CORE (1976)
KING KONG (1976)*
THE CRATER LAKE MONSTER (1977)*
THE PEOPLE THAT TIME FORGOT (1977)
PLANET OF THE DINOSAURS (1977)*
SINBAD AND THE EYE OF THE TIGER (1977)
WHERE TIME BEGAN (1978)
CAVEMAN (1981)
Q (1982)
YOR, THE HUNTER FROM THE FUTURE (1983)*
BABY (1985)
KING KONG LIVES (1986)*

APPENDIX 2:
JAPANESE FEATURE FILM CHECKLIST

Live-action Japanese feature films depicting prehistoric animals. Listed chronologically by year of U.S. release. All titles listed are the U.S. release titles (NOTE: of the titles listed here, only five--GODZILLA, KING OF THE MONSTERS, GIGANTIS, THE FIRE MONSTER, RODAN, KING KONG VS. GODZILLA and GODZILLA 1985--are discussed in this book.

GODZILLA, KING OF THE MONSTERS (1956)
RODAN (1958)
GIGANTIS, THE FIRE MONSTER (1959)
MOTHRA (1962)
VARAN, THE UNBELIEVABLE (1962)
ATRAGON (1963)
FRANKENSTEIN CONQUERS THE WORLD (1964)
GODZILLA VS. THE THING (1964)
GHIDRA, THE THREE-HEADED MONSTER (1965)
MONSTER ZERO (1965)
GAMMERA THE INVINCIBLE (1966)
GODZILLA VS. THE SEA MONSTER (1966)
WAR OF THE MONSTERS (1966)
MONSTER FROM A PREHISTORIC PLANET (1967)
THE RETURN OF THE GIANT MONSTERS (1967)
SON OF GODZILLA (1967)
YONGARY, MONSTER FROM THE DEEP (1967)
DESTROY ALL MONSTERS (1968)
DESTROY ALL PLANETS (1968)
KING KONG ESCAPES (1968)
ATTACK OF THE GIANT MONSTERS (1969)
GODZILLA's REVENGE (1969)
GAMMERA VS. MONSTER X (1970)
GAMMERA VS. ZIGRA (1971)
GODZILLA VS. THE SMOG MONSTER (1971)

GODZILLA ON MOSTER ISLAND (1972)
GODZILLA VS. MEGALON (1974)
GODZILLA VS. THE BIONIC MONSTER (1975)
TERROR OF MECHAGODZILLA (1976)
THE LEGEND OF DINOSAURS AND MONSTER BIRDS (1977)
GODZILLA 1985 (1985)

NAME INDEX

(underlined page numbers indicate illustrations)

TITLE INDEX

(underlined page numbers indicate illustrations)